GET
REAL
ABOUT
BRANDING

GET
REAL
ABOUT
BRANDING

How You Can Build Sales and Brand
Value Without Spending a Fortune on
Marketing, Advertising and Branding

ART FORWARD

GET REAL ABOUT BRANDING
HOW YOU CAN BUILD SALES AND BRAND
VALUE WITHOUT SPENDING A FORTUNE ON
MARKETING, ADVERTISING AND BRANDING

iUniverse books may be ordered through booksellers or by contacting:

*iUniverse
1663 Liberty Drive
Bloomington, IN 47403
www.iuniverse.com
1-800-Authors (1-800-288-4677)*

*ISBN: 978-1-5320-5660-4 (sc)
ISBN: 978-1-5320-5661-1 (e)*

Print information available on the last page.

iUniverse rev. date: 07/02/2019

CONTENTS

Author's Biography..vii

Introduction...xi

GET REAL Tools xxix

Step 1 –   Identify Interview Sources 1

Step 2 –   Interview Associates and Customers...........10

Step 3 –   Analyze Interviews.......................................26

Step 4 –   Identify Brand Benefit.................................30

Step 5 –   Define Your Compelling Focus....................33

Step 6 –   Create Your Brand Promise.........................38

Step 7 –   Define Your Brand Proof 45

Step 8 –   Ask the Compelling Focus Question...........53

Step 9 –   Build Repeat Sales and Referrals.................58

Step 10 – Select the Right Communications 62

Step 11 – Set Goals That Motivate Associates 83

Step 12 – Involve All Associates...................................89

Conclusion 107

Glossary of Process Terms 109

Worksheets...115

Appendix 139

AUTHOR'S BIOGRAPHY

Art Forward — president of Forward Consulting, author of *GET REAL About Branding*, developer of the GET REAL Process and consultant to dozens of successful organizations —spent more than thirty years perfecting the GET REAL Process and applying it effectively at organizations ranging from small local firms to multinational conglomerates to government entities to charitable organizations.

His global clients include Brunswick Billiards (premiere billiards tables), Boston Whaler (unsinkable recreational and work boats) and Bush Hog (a regional agricultural products company that he helped grow into a national and international brand with sales in every state as well as countries across the world.)

His local and regional clients include a homebuilding firm that boosted its profits by saving thousands of dollars in advertising expenses by getting more than 50 percent of its sales from customer referrals, a legal firm that prospered and merged with a much larger firm, a district attorney's office that sped up justice by slashing the time taken to handle cases while steering young people away from crime and saving the lives of abandoned infants in all 50 states, and a medical practice that grew consistently and sold for a premium price.

His event clients include the Senior Bowl (rebranded as the Cradle of the NFL) that went from facing the threat of termination to a sellout phenomenon with a new television contract and sell-out audiences in just six months.

Art knows how to learn what customers need and how to help businesses, professional practices, and other organizations succeed by providing it. He named and uses the American Business Advantage, which is available for free to all Americans, and makes its benefits available to you through the Process.

Art has marketing, advertising, and branding experience in fields as diverse as aircraft, refractory products, centrifuges, television equipment, industrial products, law, farm equipment, landscaping products, landscape services, building materials, boats, financial products, homebuilding, engineering services, medical services, and law enforcement.

Developed from his first-hand experience, the Process produces increased sales, effectiveness, efficiency, and profitability while building brand value and controlling marketing costs.

Art's value to his clients is illustrated by his long-term client relationships. One multi-million-dollar manufacturing company used his services continuously for more than thirty years. Another long-term client saved hundreds of thousands of dollars in advertising costs by replacing traditional media with word-of-mouth. Another increased worldwide sales of recreational products by 40 percent in two years. All avoided the expensive pitfalls hidden in many marketing, advertising, and branding methods.

Art gets involved with his clients. He demonstrated new aircraft performance to aviation writers, went into an annealing furnace to learn about insulation applications, worked with farmers to learn their equipment needs and test products, faced rough seas with offshore fishermen to determine what they needed in new boat designs, worked with bank employees to learn how to unleash more of their talents, and perfected a new home demonstration method that motivated homebuyers to provide hundreds of referrals. These experiences and more illustrate the Process.

Over the last few years, Art adapted the Process so others can use it to grow sales, build brand value, and continue to find success long after their founders move on.

INTRODUCTION

The key to building sales and a powerful brand without spending a fortune is to know what your customers need now, promise and prove you will deliver it, and then make sure your customers understand the value you provided as you ask them for more business or referrals.

Your opportunity to benefit from this is huge. Many organizations have lost focus on their real purpose: <u>meeting current customer needs.</u> You can capitalize on that.

At many organizations, owners, managers, and associates don't agree on the current needs of their customers, much less how to meet them. This lack of focus on meeting current customer needs means you have room to leap ahead of the competition by differentiating your products, services, or brand. It is also your opportunity to save thousands, perhaps millions, of dollars that would otherwise be wasted on undisciplined creativity in marketing, advertising, and branding (i.e. expensive logos and taglines that are unrelated to meeting customer needs or are changed often).

The GET REAL Process shows you how to profit from these opportunities. It teaches how to capture the ideas and insights of associates and customers with thought-provoking questions, as well as how to put the answers to work, making your organization, products, and services unique.

The Process plugs you and your organization into the creativity and enthusiasm of the succeed-for-their-own-benefit thinking of Americans. Whatever your business, profession, or organization and whatever your role in it, the business of your organization is to meet your customers' needs better than your competitors. You need to make sure your customers know that both before and after the sale. Recognize and respond to customers' current needs and you will prosper; you will sail past the thousands of organizations that allow computer modeling and the replacement of the communication of useful information with fancy logos, slogans, and standardized business practices that may make them look just like their competitors.

The most remarkable thing about meeting customers' needs is that your associates and customers will tell you all you need to know about their needs and how to meet them . . . for free. The information you need is waiting for you in the hearts and minds of your associates and customers, and will be for years to come. The Process will help you access this information and use it to build sales and long-lasting brand value.

The Process will help you succeed in these challenging times by:

- Identifying all your customers (both traditional and new types of customers)
- Identifying your customers' current needs
- Capturing your ideas
- Analyzing input and identifying insights
- Promising your customers and prospects that your products or services will meet their needs and proving it to them with relevant facts
- Making sure you deliver what your customers need
- Telling your customers about the value you have delivered as you ask for more business or referrals
- Collecting and using meaningful data
- Doing it year after year.

You will learn where to get valuable information, how to evaluate it, and how to use it to build sales and a powerful brand. You will also discover how to improve efficiency, create your own media, stimulate innovation, integrate marketing and sales, open new markets, and motivate associates to work efficiently and effectively.

The Process is presented in twelve steps that connect everything you do to meeting your customers' needs. Each step includes its own worksheets. As you move through the steps, use the worksheets to create and apply your own unique tools. The Step 12 worksheet incorporates your work in the previous worksheets into your Associate Involvement/Communication Plan, which will motivate your associates and customers for years to come.

There's no question that it's tougher to compete today than it was twenty years ago—a surplus of choice, instant information, imports from cheap labor markets, more competition, similar products and services offered, and many other challenges stand in your way.

But many entrepreneurs, managers, and professionals make it tougher than it has to be because they don't put the uniting overall purpose of their organization (meeting customers' current needs) first. Instead, they get distracted by (and spend money on) technology, marketing, advertising, branding, and standardized business practices without first ensuring that these new elements will help meet customers' needs.

Technology, marketing, advertising, and branding, as well as standardized business practices, can be expensive and ineffective when they are applied without a focus on the real *business* of the business. American businesses invest millions in these new aspects but do little to make them work together to meet the unique needs of their customers.

The results can be appalling. Here are some examples:

A two hundred-million-dollar manufacturing business bought and installed powerful technology, adopted a highly-touted standardized manufacturing system, and replaced management that had produced profits and growth for decades. Meeting customer needs took a back seat. After a few years, sales were down substantially, profits disappeared, and the company was put up for sale.

A famous boat manufacturer ignored the fact its unsinkable advantage was offered by other boat manufacturers and let its leadership position in technology and innovative design slip.

A nationally-televised football bowl game concentrated so much on rewarding its volunteers that it lost its stadium and television audiences.

A billiards table manufacturer stagnated as it focused on its traditional male customer base, even though women decide what furniture comes into their homes.

Technology, marketing, advertising, branding, and standardized business practices without the discipline of serving associate and customer needs can destroy the vital difference customers use to distinguish between your organization and your competitors. They can be part of the problem rather than part of the solution.

Success today depends on harnessing everything you and your associates do to meet current customer needs. To do this, you must know your customers' motivations, their perceptions of their needs, and their current thinking. You will learn these secrets and how to use them to create success now and in the future as you complete the twelve Process worksheets.

I created the Process over more than thirty years of helping organizations build sales and brand value. These organizations ranged from single individuals to giant conglomerates. I used the Process to help me and my clients understand customers' current needs, focus on meeting them, and get credit for doing it. The worksheets guided us. The Process evolved and improved as I updated it with my experiences and the experiences of my clients. Recently, I documented it and added more examples from my career as well as explanations of the Process's foundations so that entrepreneurs, managers, and professionals can use it.

In my consulting practice, I encourage clients to do everything they can themselves because that is how they learn. My objective is to make them successful now and equip them for long-term success. I am available to help, but I encourage them to participate in the process themselves. In this way, they will be motivated by their business needs as well as their desire to make the Process pay off. My experience is that the Process enhances professional life as it improves business results.

At the heart of the Process is learning your customers' current needs and utilizing your thinking, your associates' thinking, and your customers' thinking to meet them. You will learn who to ask for valuable ideas and insights in Step 1 and what questions to ask and how to ask them in Step 2.

Successful salespeople know the value of their ideas and insights and other peoples' ideas and insights. They learn to listen to customers and ask questions. Unfortunately, the use of this information is often limited to individual salespeople. The Process makes the input and insights of associates and customers pay off for everyone in the organization, as well as their customers.

Learning current associate and customer needs and utilizing your thinking and theirs to meet them can be a huge boon for businesses, professional firms, and other organizations as our society goes through huge changes. Lots of information about marketing, advertising, and branding exists, but most of it won't apply to your specific situation. The ideas and insights of your associates and customers—who are on the scene dealing with changes that affect them and their organizations every day—are what you need to know and use. They are current and can make a huge difference if you learn and apply them. As things change, ideas and insights change, only your associates and customers can keep you ahead of the game.

The American Business Advantage—
A Special Opportunity

Learning current customer and associate needs and meeting them can present special opportunities for American businesses, professional firms, non-profits, government agencies, and other organizations.

This is because learning and responding to your customers' needs taps into the DNA of Americans. They grow up with the freedom to be self-interested. Most Americans see things in terms of how those things will affect them personally. They are motivated to think and reach their own conclusions rather than just move with the herd. That means most of them recognize, think about, and learn to cope with change in their personal lives and their work. Their input and insights are valuable. The Process helps you access and use their knowledge and experience to build your success as well as theirs.

In the pages ahead, you will learn:

- How to build a lasting, valuable brand based on delivering what customers need now
- Where to get ideas and insights
- How to identify the most valuable information
- How to put valuable information to work for yourself and your business, professional firm, government agency, non-profit, or other organization
- How to harness advancements in technology, communication, and business practices to meet current customer needs
- How to make your customers see your people, products, and services as better than those of your competitors
- How to make sure your customers know about the difference between your products or services and those of your competitors

- How to use the difference between you and your competitors to trigger more sales, more repeat sales, more referrals, more brand value, and more profit
- How to turn the power of knowing and consistently meeting customers' needs and telling your customers when you do it into your own powerful—and free—media.

Before you start the process, let's review some of the current realities of today's business environment that make focusing on meeting customers' needs with the help of your associates and customers a necessity as well as your best opportunity.

It's All about What People Need "Now"

"Now" is a moment in time or a period of time. For organizations that exist to serve other people's needs, "now" is a span of time in which customers' motivations inform their beliefs and guide decisions. In modern times, motivations, beliefs, and decisions change constantly as reality and perceptions are affected by experiences, news broadcasts, events, digital communication, and hundreds of other influencers.

A few years ago, much of the world, including the United States of America, experienced a "Now Period," during which "quick" was more important than "right," money was the key measure of success, "complicated" was better than "simple," credit was better than cash, use of technology was more important than providing service, want was considered more important than need, branding with logos and slogans was more important than delivering value, and adopting standardized business practices was more important than creating unique customer benefits. Then things changed.

The real estate and housing boom collapsed, mortgage loans went into default, mortgage-backed securities collapsed, the United States Congress spent billions in a matter of days, financial scandals made fortunes disappear, unemployment soared, and bankruptcies set new records. On the heels of these developments, government debt soared; the government expanded; the lines between news, advertising, and entertainment blurred; and costs rose. The economy suffered and has spent the last decade coming back to life. These events and many others along the same lines changed the motivations, beliefs, and decisions of your associates and customers.

Change isn't unusual; it is normal and constant. But these changes were bigger than most. They appeared to be sudden. They were profound and widespread. They couldn't be met with gradual adjustments. They affected the motivations and thinking of millions of people. They created a new "Now Period" of perception that swept over us suddenly. To successfully navigate today's "Now Period," you must know what these changes wrought and what they are doing now to the beliefs and decisions of your associates and customers. Only then can you respond to them.

The current motivations and thoughts of your associates and customers aren't in books and reports. They aren't taught in business schools. They contain too much emotion to be captured in textbooks and standard reports. They change fast. They are complex. They live and evolve in your associates' and customers' minds and hearts, moment by moment.

Your customers know that their thinking, feelings, and needs are changing. They live and work with the changes every day. They accommodate them. From their first-hand experiences, they conceive the best ideas and insights into how they (and you) must adjust to change. They figure it out because they have to. They, and your associates or contacts, are the best sources of information on how to make your organization successful today and in the future. They can tell you what they need now, what will convince them you have it, how to communicate with them, how to tell them you have delivered what they need, and how to ask for more business.

"Trust" Is the New Motivation

Until recently, "want" dominated motivation in developed countries. Many people believed they were beyond having to deal with need. They wanted to:

- Have everything *now*
- Look good
- Be high-status
- Be admired
- Be rich
- Assume the "personality" of their car
- Show their boss how quickly they could finish an assignment
- Dazzle their associates with "what ifs"
- Get credit for saving money on shortcuts even if they short-change customers
- Use technology to achieve the same results being achieved by competitors
- Slash costs without first identifying and protecting "the goose that laid the golden egg"
- Camouflage risks with unrealistic projections
- Jump at the "quick fix"
- Replace human emotions with statistics
- Ignore information that appeared to stand in their way
- Have all the answers instantly.

"Want" was paramount. More was good. Quick was good. The use of new technology, marketing, advertising, branding, and standardized business practices and methods of thinking were ends unto themselves.

I saw it in our consulting practice. Managers called with requests that emphasized speed and exaggeration of expectations rather than results. "Never mind making sure it matches with our situation, just tell me about something exciting I can recommend at my meeting tomorrow," one said.

Some managers focused on imitation and the false concept that all customers are the same. They didn't look beyond statistics or into how ideas can be applied to different people. They ignored human emotions and experiences. They were in a hurry to get what they wanted rather than to deliver what their customers needed. It wasn't unusual for managers changing jobs to describe a year or two at one company as "a nice run."

It is different today for consumers and businesses.

Today's consumers know they were tricked and that they, not the tricksters, paid for it. Many lost their homes. Others lost their jobs. Many foreign-made products failed quickly or never worked as expected. Reliable brands put their logos on products that fell apart. Executives of charities received huge salaries and bonuses to ask for your money and were not careful about how they spent it. Disappointment and anger spread across the country. Trust became a valuable and seemingly rare commodity. The reality of "You get what you pay for" and "Buyer beware" sank in.

Consumers no longer believe their needs are met by empty promises. They are no longer focused on just their wants or just getting it done quickly. Their needs are too real and too imminent. Now they need to:

- Make real contributions to hold onto a job
- Get a practical education that leads to a career, even if they have to be re-educated
- Use their car for transportation rather than as a status symbol
- Protect their investments and savings rather than gamble with them
- Pay off loans to stop interest costs
- Save up and pay with cash
- Live within their means

- Buy only what they need
- Serve their employees rather than themselves

Many businesses and other organizations haven't adjusted to the deep skepticism prevalent today. The fact is that people just don't believe empty promises anymore. Today, businesses and other organizations need to:

- Identify and meet current customer needs
- Build profitable sales
- Build brand value
- Understand and minimize risk
- Create and deliver added value for their traditional customers
- Identify and serve the needs of new customers
- Capture and use the knowledge and experience of associations and customers
- Make sure their promises are believable
- Keep their promises
- Show their customers they keep their promises
- Satisfy customers so they will buy again
- Deliver more value to customers than their competitors
- Communicate the delivery of value better than their competitors
- Provide good experiences for their customers
- Make sure their customers recognize the benefits their products or services provide
- Cut organizational fat without cutting muscle
- Find more efficient ways of doing things
- Get more repeat sales and referrals
- Wring value for their customers from technology and business practices as well as advantages for their businesses
- Use traditional and new media and other communication techniques to communicate the benefits they deliver to customers

- Use new business practices and technologies to create increased value for customers, not just to reduce costs
- Create their own effective media
- Equip their associates to "self-motivate" themselves and each other
- Provide their associates with a way to make the right decisions
- Build brands that produce long-term dividends for shareholders and substantial value when it is time to sell the business
- Build trust through every contact with customers.

"Trust" has always been a business asset. It is more than that today; it is *the* business asset. Bombarded by an almost incalculable number of sales messages on the street, on TV, on the internet, and on social media, people in business and their customers have their shields up. Promises alone won't do it anymore. Meeting real needs by keeping promises and making sure customers and potential customers know it are today's ways to success. These two steps build trust over and over until it is part of your firm's identity. The Process shows you how to do this consistently year after year.

Your Success Depends on Other People

The change in motivation from want to need and the growing importance of trust was dramatic. Less obvious but just as important is the growing dependence of professionals on other people for their success. More than at any other time in history, success depends on other people. There is too much to know to make it on your own.

Christopher Columbus probably knew how to do every task on his ships, from sewing up a torn sail to navigating. The captain of a modern ship commands a more complex vessel. He or she is unlikely to know how to replace a worn bearing or fix the software in the

GPS navigation system or engine controls. The captain's success is determined by the crew as well as other specialists who develop, install, and maintain the ship's systems. The modern captain needs other people to compete successfully in the worldwide transportation industry and survive at sea.

My own experience—and I suspect yours—is the same. I need help. Before I wrote this introduction, I was on the phone with the firm that hosts our website and email account. Their expert helped me adjust settings that restored our interrupted email in a few minutes.

Today, success is largely determined by your associates. You need their help. To get it, you must know what they consider success and help them achieve it.

The most independent people I've met in business—field sales reps—have known for decades that they need help to succeed. Traveling with field sales reps over the years, I learned that the most successful ones cultivate other associates who can help them deliver on their promises to customers. These people hold many different jobs: customer service, shipping, credit, sales management, accounting, product service, parts, engineering, and others.

Never before has cooperation been as valuable.

Harness the First-Hand Experience of Involved People

The Process equips you to put the experience and thinking of involved people to work. Gathering and analyzing the experience and thinking of involved people—people with first-hand experience of your business—is immensely valuable today. Associates, customers, and new customer types can all contribute experience and thinking to the Process, through interviews, ongoing contact, tools, and the Associate Involvement/Communication Plan you create in Step 12. The Process guides this thinking, analyzes it, and puts the most valuable of that information to work.

No Silver Bullets

Buying and re-buying decisions are where the rubber meets the road for most organizations. It's obvious for businesses and professionals, but it's also true for other organizations.

Schools try to get students to "buy" knowledge with their time, energy, and money. Politicians try to get citizens to "buy" legislation and programs with promises of a better society. Charities try to convince potential contributors to "buy" good feelings with contributions. Almost every organization has something it wants to sell.

People rarely make buying decisions based on only one factor. They decide based on many factors, some of which you and your associates can influence. Some of these factors are factual, others are emotional. To succeed today, you must know the factors you can influence better than your competitors. They add up to reputation.

You have many opportunities to show customers how your organization meets their needs: products, product features, services, advertising, website, sales literature, sales promotion, point-of-sale, pricing, signage, sales conversations, videos, packaging, delivery, phone contacts, your associates' actions and attitudes, and others. Literally every contact with customers is an opportunity. Many are wasted. Some may work against you. These opportunities—both the good and bad experiences of customers—add up to a positive, negative, or entirely absent perception of your organization and its ability to deliver what your customers need.

Getting and Evaluating Input

Organizations are made up of people, not just business models. Customers are people, not statistics. Successful individuals and organizations are people focused on learning and meeting the needs of others.

The Process helps you put what makes organizations work—the power of people meeting current customer needs—into or back into your business, professional firm, or other organization. This power is based on the first-hand experience of people in many fields. It is logical. It is presented in easy-to-understand language. It is designed to meet today's changing business and professional environment. It is focused on getting your job done right—not just telling you what other people did. It is practical. It contains no long explanations, diagrams, or complex theories; just practical, successful concepts and real-life experiences of them.

The terms used in the Process are simple and intuitive. The glossary helps make sure you, your associates, and your customers are clear about what these terms mean. Use the definitions to keep you, your associates, and your customers on the same page.

Getting input and insights from associates and customers is important; so is capturing your thinking. You will do both as you work through the 12 Steps.

Organizing the input and insights you acquire and choosing the right ones to use is vital and begins during interviews with associates and customers. The Process suggests six categories to help you obtain and evaluate information:

1 – Traditional and new customer types
2 – Their different needs
3 – Your capabilities
4 – Communication
5 – Customer benefits
6 – Your input

Categorizing input and insights helps you capture and select the most useful information to put to work. Your application of the Process will link every step you and your associates take to meeting current customer needs and will make sure you get credit with customers for doing it.

The process taps into the value of people. It helps you learn and use their motivations and thinking (as well as yours) to identify current customer needs and the best ways to meet them. It takes into account emotions, feelings, and other factors that can't be reduced to numbers or standard reports.

This establishes or re-establishes associates and customers as people, not statistics. It inspires business strategies and implementation driven by what customers need and associates want to deliver. It ensures your organization serves your customers' current needs and makes your products, services, and brand unique for reasons that are important to customers and difficult for your competitors to imitate.

Based on Experience, Not Theory

Experience is important when dealing with other people. They relate to it. The individual steps of the Process are illustrated with examples from my experience building sales and brands simultaneously. These examples are in italics. Use them to further your understanding of the Process and stimulate your thinking. Cite my experiences to your associates and customers to stimulate their thinking and help them understand how they can benefit.

Over thirty years of my career has been condensed into the Process. But that's just a small part of the experience it captures; it also represents hundreds of years of the applied experiences of my clients and their customers. People who contributed are consumers, business owners, managers, executives, salespeople, investors, attorneys, customer service reps, sales reps, purchasing agents, distributor associates, dealer associates, sales and service personnel, buyers, financial experts, nurses, office managers, physicians, and patients. Their experiences include raising families, enjoying a hobby, managing a home, and making a living.

These people include:

- The board chairman of an international aircraft manufacturer who taught me to remember a primary motivation of people who purchase general aviation airplanes
- The editor who gave me my first clues on how to probe for real motivation, proactive thinking, forgotten facts, and insights
- The lawyer who built a practice defending malpractice lawsuits by paying attention to the needs of the families of the physicians he defended, as well as the case
- The mortgage loan processor who inspired the staff of a Honolulu bank to grow their business and profits with a trip to the airport
- The bank teller who, equipped with her lawn mower, showed her associates how they could help quadruple their bank's assets by cutting the grass around an ATM over a weekend
- The retired surgeon who, after moving to the country, bought a horse and used a lawn mower to cut her pasture
- The customer service rep who remembered a forgotten research project that we used to help drive a huge sales increase for an international company
- The female executive who took up pool because she could outplay her burly boyfriend
- The international engineering firm president who kept notes of thanks from employees and customers in his "feel good" file.

Your Thinking Is Valuable—Don't Let It Get Away

Your thinking is valuable. Your associates' thinking is valuable. Your customers' thinking is valuable. The Process makes this thinking even more valuable by eliciting more of it, capturing it, categorizing it, analyzing it, selecting the best of it, and putting it to work.

Let's get to work. Read through the twelve steps first. As you do, jot down your thoughts and insights about your work, business, or profession as they come to mind, and try to incorporate these observations with points raised by the twelve steps. Then work through the Process using the worksheets (or subscribe to the web-based software and let it do the sorting and grouping). Remember that the thinking you do as you decide how to classify associate and customer input and insights is important in order to acquire the benefits of your associates' and customers' knowledge and experience; it will focus all the actions you and your associates perform on meeting current customer needs. Use what you learn to differentiate your business, professional practice, government agency, non-profit, or other organization and make it more successful. Keep it successful by interviewing associates and customers every few years and making necessary adjustments to the steps.

Assistance is available to jump-start your efforts and support you as you work through the process. Learn about it at our website www.getrealprocess.com. Use the contact link to tell us about your situation.

You may want to use our web-based GET REAL Process Software to expedite your work and give your associates a way to capture what they learn day by day. You can try it at www.getrealprocess.com. The software will save at least 50 percent of your time as it does all the sorting and grouping for you and makes decisions about subjects such as media selection easy.

GET REAL TOOLS

Before beginning the steps in the process familiarize yourself and your associates with the GET REAL Tools that you will create and use:

Brand Benefit is the overarching benefit your products, services, associates, and brand provide.

Brand Promise is your promise that your products, services, associates, and brand deliver your Brand Benefit to customers.

Brand Proof is facts that prove your products, services, associates, and brand keep your Brand Promise for traditional and new customers.

Compelling Focus helps define how you and your associates behave so as to consistently deliver your Brand Benefit to customers.

Compelling Focus Question helps you and your associates ask themselves and each other how their decisions help implement your Compelling Focus.

External Media Analysis and Readiness Chart helps you choose effective exterior media and communication techniques and make sure they are in place before launching programs.

Internal Media Analysis and Readiness Chart helps you choose effective internal media and other communication techniques and use them to support programs.

Input and Analysis Chart helps you identify useful information during interviews, select the most important insights, and understand the relationships between individual pieces of information.

Pitfall Alarms help you identify marketing, advertising and branding pitfalls before they cost money and waste time.

STEP 1

Identify Interview Sources

Step 1 of the Process identifies associates and customers who can share their input and insights in six information categories:

1. CUST – traditional and new customers types
2. NEED – traditional and new customer types' current needs
3. CAPS – your organization's capability to meet customers' needs, as well as capabilities you may decide to add
4. COMS – communication in terms of information that can generate sales, repeat sales, and referrals, as well as the media and materials/methods that will deliver it
5. BENS – benefits customers will pay for
6. YOUR – your input.

Human motivation is driven by many experiences seen through individual eyes and transformed by individual intellects and feelings. It is affected by news, advertising, relationships, conversations, travel, sermons, talk shows, gossip, books, movies, videos, social media, conversations, emotions, and countless other influencers. It is complex and personal. Unless you have a way to understand your customers' experiences from their points of view, you can't know their needs and respond to them effectively and consistently.

Standard research is valuable, but it doesn't meet your needs fully. It is unusual for it to elicit responses that aren't just at the "top of mind." It can't account for all the factors influencing your customers. It can't get into associates and customers' minds far enough to reveal what they are thinking and feeling. Even when questions are carefully prepared and asked and the answers accurately recorded and scientifically analyzed, useful conclusions and actionable results remain elusive. Insights are rare.

The reason is simple. Most research subjects give quick responses to standard research questions without thinking. They have little or no motivation to contribute valuable information. There is little or nothing in it for them—nothing new to learn, nothing to stimulate new ideas, nothing that will benefit them or make their jobs or lives easier or their futures brighter. Their only motivation is to get the interview or questionnaire finished as soon as possible, so they give quick, easy answers, usually with little thought.

Reviews and discussions of the information provided by standard research often produce few useful insights. That's because input based on quick responses doesn't reveal what customers are thinking when they actually *are* thinking. Ineffective strategies result because they are not based on what customers really believe. In addition, few if any parameters are used to review this input, organize it, analyze it, and put it to work.

To learn motivations, get insights, and put those insights to work, you need your associates and customers to do some of the thinking for you. You must have their input and insights. You must know their needs, how their needs are changing, and how your organization can meet those changing needs. You need to know what capabilities your organization has or could have that can help it meet your customers' needs better than your competitors. You need to know the information customers need and the media they will use to get it. Finally, you need to know the benefits they will pay for.

How to Select Associates for Interviews

Associates who work with customers or who assist or manage other associates who work with customers (or others who have a useful view of your organization) are your best sources for information about your customers' needs. Use those associates with customer contact to help you choose associates and others to interview.

Examples of associate positions with customer contact:

1. Business
   a. Managers who work with associates with customer contact or have direct customer contact themselves
   b. Directors
   c. Associates who have contact with distributors/dealers and or customers. These could be involved in:
      i. Outside sales
      ii. Inside sales
      iii. Customer service
      iv. Order receipt
      v. Credit management
      vi. Shipping
      vii. Buyers for retail

   d. Associates who field calls from sales reps and customers

2. Higher education
   a. Administrators
   b. Trustees
   c. Business office associates
   d. Deans

     e. Admissions directors
     f. Career counselors
     g. Professors
     h. Coaches

3. Medical (understand and follow HIPPA law)
   a. Physicians
   b. Highly trained professionals such as embryologists
   c. Nurses
   d. Office managers
   e. Administrative staff who have patient contact
   f. Insurance coordinators

4. Legal
   a. Attorneys
   b. Paralegals

5. Public accountants
   a. Certified public accountants
   b. Support accountants

6. Government
   a. Elected officials
   b. Appointed officials
   c. Managers of departments
   d. Associates who serve citizens

Characteristics of associates that can be helpful:

- People who get results
- People who make suggestions
- People with years of experience on the job
- People who care about the organization and its customers
- People who submit ideas or point out opportunities

- People who bring up problems and offer solutions
- People who will tell you what they think and work with you to find solutions to problems or ways to utilize opportunities
- People who believe your organization provides value to customers, communities, or other stakeholders
- People who believe your organization could provide more value to customers, communities or other stakeholders.

Examples of associates for interviews:

- *Associates interviewed for a medical practice included physicians, embryologists, nurses, and office staff*
- *Associates interviewed for a pool table manufacturer included managers, dealers, customer service representatives, and salespeople.*
- *Associates interviewed for a national football bowl game included NFL players and coaches, local government officials and leaders, event committee members, the executive director, volunteers, half-time coordinator, NFL players and coaches and television producer.*

Following interviews, thank interviewees for their time during interviews by email.

How to Select Customers for Interviews

Customers who either buy your products/services or who influence decisions to buy them are your other primary source of valuable information and insights. Use the criteria below to select customer interview candidates and ask them to suggest other candidates. Provide feedback to customers interviewed through individual letters or emails thanking them for their time and citing examples of their input.

Individuals who buy or influence purchase of products/services:

1. Businesses to Business
   a. Owner(s)
   b. Purchasing professionals
   c. Administrators
   d. Product managers
   e. Service employees
   f. Salespeople
   g. General managers
   h. Engineers
   i. Supply chain workers
   j. Division managers
   k. Department managers
   l. Buyers
   m. People who could make referrals or place additional orders

2. Distributors/dealers
   a. Owner(s)
   b. Salespeople
   c. Service employees
   d. Coordinators or office managers

3. Higher education
   a. Prospective students
   b. Parents of prospective students
   c. Students who attended the school or now attend it
   d. Parents whose children attended the school or now attend it
   e. High school guidance counselors
   f. Coaches
   g. Clergy
   h. Recruiters

      i.   Siblings of students

      j.   Friends

      k. Alumni

4. Medical (understand and follow HIPAA laws)
   a. Patients
   b. Patients' families
   c. People who influence patients
   d. Referring physicians
   e. People you would like to have as patients

5. Legal
   a. Clients
   b. Clients' associates
   c. Clients' families
   d. People who influence clients
   e. People you would like to have as clients
   f. People who use legal services frequently
   g. People who use legal services occasionally

6. Public accountants
7. Clients you have now
8. Clients you would like to have
9. Government
   a. Citizens
   b. Organizations of citizens
   c. Citizens who interact with government
   d. Business and professional people who interact with government employees

10. Retail
    a. Consumers
    b. Spouses of consumers
    c. Families of consumers

    d.   Friends of consumers

    e.   People perceived as knowledgeable by consumers

    f.   Other influencers of consumers

    g.   People who follow products such as cars, fashions, and food

    h.   Owners of the same or similar products

    i.   Users of the same or similar products

    j.   People who could buy from you

Characteristics of customers who can provide valuable information:

- People who will tell you the truth
- People who offer information and/or make suggestions
- People with years of experience with your products or services
- People who are new to your products and services
- People who bring up problems
- People who research purchases thoroughly
- People who have yet to buy from you
- People with experience using your products or services

Examples of customers for interviews

- *Customers interviewed for a college included corporate recruiters and the human resource manager for a school that recruits education majors.*
- *Customers interviewed for a pool table manufacturer included players, a billiards parlor manager, professional men and women, mothers of teenagers, and homeowners.*
- *Customers interviewed for the national football bowl game included fans, television audience members, citizens of the local community, NFL coaches, scouts, and players.*

Seek private interviews so you can follow a line of questioning and ask your interviewees to elaborate on their answers. Accept phone interviews only when in-person interviews can't be arranged. Ask for a forty-five-minute appointment. You'll find that interview candidates often extend the length of their appointments.

Explain to prospective interviewees that you are seeking to better understand associates' and customers' needs as you recognize that they change from time to time. The benefit for associates is the opportunity to contribute to making processes better and the recognition that comes with it. The benefit for customers is the opportunity to help your organization better meet their needs and their organizations' needs.

The information categories will help you decide which associates and customers to interview, but you should also consider their training and experience. The information categories will also help you assist interviewees in making worthwhile contributions.

The discipline of the Process is provided by the worksheets; they help you and everyone involved stay on track to build sales and brand value year after year. They guide your thinking.

Review the categories of information you will seek in interviews before each meeting. Then use the Step 1 worksheets to schedule and track interviews.

Remember: include management in associate interviews.

Set aside at least an hour to interview yourself using the categories and questions as your guides. This is a very important and continuous step throughout the Process. It's important because you will be the person most exposed to all the first-hand thinking that is elicited, documented, analyzed, and put to work.

Use the Step 1 worksheet in the Worksheets section at the back of this book to identify associates and customers for interviews.

STEP 2

Interview Associates and Customers

Interview techniques are the same for associates and customers. Questions are somewhat different between the groups. Sincerity, honesty, and interest are the keys to establishing confidence in your interviewees that you want to make a difference for them and their organizations. For associates, this difference is the level of satisfaction and recognition they receive from their work and their own effectiveness. For customers, it's improvements in the benefits they or their firms receive from your organization's products or services. Your sincerity, honesty, and interest are communicated by your demeanor as well as by the interview questions.

Successful interviewing is driven by practice, the ability to share experiences interviewees can relate to, and careful listening. Interviewers who value other people in all positions can learn the motivations and needs of their associates and customers as well as generate and recognize insights. You can be successful at interviews by using the following interviewing techniques and questions, projecting a sincere interest in learning from interviewees, and citing appropriate examples (presented here in italics).

Use these interviewing techniques with associates and customers:

- Wear similar clothing to the people you're interviewing.
- Pledge to yourself that you will do no harm to the people you interview through anything you say or do, and keep your word. Promise confidentially and live up to it when interviewees request it.
- Share appropriate examples from *GET REAL About Branding* or examples from your own experiences to help interviewees understand the input you are seeking and the importance of their participation in ensuring the success of the Process. Stress too the ways in which they and their organizations will benefit.
- Share some information as it develops so interviewees feel they are learning and are stimulated by the ideas you are capturing.
- Test information you received in previous interviews.
- Ask the same questions in several different ways to make sure interviewees understand them and are thinking about their answers.
- Give interviewees plenty of time to formulate their answers.
- Repeat back key parts of what interviewees say to make sure you understand what they are saying, check accuracy, and elicit further information.
- Be sensitive to the interviewee's comfort level as you ask questions (don't ask questions in ways that make them feel uncomfortable or pursue questions they seem to want to avoid).
- Assure interviewees there are no right or wrong answers.

Questions for associates and customers are designed to elicit input and insights into the six categories of current information.

Ask for information about what is relevant to both traditional and new customers. Treat the interview like a conversation and give the interviewee plenty of time to formulate answers and talk.

Interview associates first. The information you learn from them is important and will help you elicit valuable information during your customer interviews. Customers can verify and expand on information you learned from associates. They can give you input and insights available nowhere else.

Ask open-ended questions of associates, such as:

- Who are our traditional customers? (Explain that, in the Process, customers can be anyone you or your associates can provide with benefits.)
- Who are our new customers?
- Who influences different types of customers and how do you or our associates benefit (or could benefit) them?
- What do our traditional customers need now and how have these needs changed?
- What capabilities does our organization have (or could it have) to meet customers' traditional needs?
- What capabilities does our organization have (or could it have) to meet customers' new needs?
- What capabilities would help you and our associates be more effective?
- What information do our customers need to know about our organization before and after they buy and what communication techniques do they (or could they) rely on to receive this information?
- What information do our customers need to know about our products or services and what communication techniques do they (or could they) rely on to receive it?
- What information or capabilities do you have (or could you have) to prove our organization's products or services

meet our different customers' needs and how should this information be communicated to customers?

- What tools do you have (or could you have) that prove our organization's products or services meet our different customers' needs (case histories, videos, facts, research, tests, etc.)?

- How do you (or could you) inform customers of the progress of their orders, services, or delivery?

- When and how do you (or could you) ask customers for repeat business or referrals?

- How do you (or could you) tell customers they have received what they ordered?

- How do you make sure (or could you make sure) our customers are satisfied when they have received our organization's products or services?

- What are the good experiences our products or services provide (or could provide) for customers?

- What media and other communication techniques do (or would) our customers pay attention to (email updates, phone updates, advertising, websites, social media)?

- What information do you need to be more effective for our customers?

- How do you know when customers have had a good experience with our organization's products or services?

- How do you remind customers of good experiences?

- How could you ask for additional business or referrals when you remind customers of good experiences with our products or services?

- What are (or could be) the benefits of our organizations' products or services and how do you (or could you) contribute to them?

- How could you assist customers in documenting the benefits of our products or services?

- What media and other communication techniques do you (or could you) use to communicate this information to other customers?
- What benefits from our products and services do customers need now compared to the recent past?
- What are (or could be) the benefits our organization delivers to its different customers?
- When do our customers realize the benefits of our products or services and how could you point them out initially and over time?
- What would help our customers understand more of the benefits our products or services provide?
- What helps you (or could help you) deliver benefits to our customers?
- How do you and your associates help (or how could you help) deliver benefits to customers using capabilities you already have or could add?
- What internal operations could be changed to help associates deliver benefits to customers?

Ask these open-ended questions of customers or people you would like to have as customers:

- What have been your traditional needs and your organization's traditional needs?
- What are your current needs and your organization's current needs?
- What does (or could) our organization do better to meet your needs or your organization's needs?
- What information do you need to make a buying decision initially and what do you need to ensure you'll remain comfortable with your decision?

- When considering a purchase, what will convince you that the right things will happen after you make a purchase, both prior to and after delivery?
- What could our organization do that would better illustrate the benefits of our products or services?
- What information would you like to receive about our organization's products, services, benefits, or applications, and how would you like to receive it?
- What motivates (or could motivate) you to buy from our organization? (Price is always a consideration—find out what else is.)
- What would motivate you to buy from our organization again or provide referrals?
- What information do you need about our organization?
- How do you decide if you will buy from the same organization again?
- What will convince you of satisfactory delivery?
- What will convince you of satisfactory performance of our products or services?
- How do you know when delivery is made and how do you decide whether it is satisfactory?
- What do you consider a good experience for you or your organization with regards to our organization, products, or services?
- What capabilities or improvements does our organization need to make to meet your current needs?
- What is the benefit our brand offers to your organization (or to you)?

Develop other questions and follow-up questions that will help you clarify points. Give interviewees a chance to think and talk. Conclude the interview when you have covered the categories of the customer's needs, capabilities, communications, and benefits, and be sure to record your own thoughts and realizations.

Don't try to ask all the questions at every interview. Be flexible. Use the questions to learn about areas where interviewees can best respond and most want to respond. Use the interviewing techniques and examples described to help interviewees understand what you are looking for, that you are sharing information they may find useful, and that you want to get the information right so their investment of time and thought pays off for them and their organizations.

It's often useful to tell interviewees how others are answering the questions as long as you don't identify them or reveal confidences. You are building a growing pool of information from the interviews that will stimulate your thinking and, when this information is shared with interviewees, it can stimulate their own thinking. Ask them for their views on information you have already gathered or ask them to expand upon it.

Encourage interviewees to think about the questions and help them formulate their answers—but don't answer the questions for them. Let them talk. Treat each interview like a discussion where both parties are learning things of interest. Review information with interviewees to clarify it; make sure it is their thinking, not yours; and give them opportunities to elaborate. Do not interrupt. They may be on the verge of telling you something important.

Take notes. If their information suggests something to you, record these observations so you don't forget them. Make sure you consider these notes when you select information to move to the Input Analysis Chart in Step 3.

Example of reviewing information to verify it and generate further input

I find it effective to say to interviewees: "I want to be sure I understand what you said. Let me repeat it back to you." Then I repeat back the information in my own words and ask if I got it right and for further clarification (i.e. "Did I hear you right when you said the spouse and family of a physician you represented in a malpractice lawsuit were also your clients? What was the benefit you created for them?").

Be sure to ask associates and customers about possible customers for your organization based on the definition of a customer as someone your organization can benefit. Don't ignore suggestions of new customers because they don't seem to fit with traditional customers; often, new customers' input, which may not appear to make sense initially, will eventually seem obvious as you review what interviewees report they or their organizations need today. Think in terms of the customers' needs your organization's products or services meet now and those they could meet in the future.

As you take notes and review those notes after interviews, mark useful information and insights (things you learned or were reminded of) with the following abbreviations to signify the six important categories:

CUST – Customers
NEED – Needs
CAPS – Capabilities
COMS – Communication
BENS – Benefits
YOUR – Your input

In Step 3, you will extract and organize the information you gathered through interviews using the Information Analysis Chart. Then you will use this chart to maintain your focus on meeting your customers' current needs.

Anything that can be used to communicate effectively with customers or deliver benefits to them is useful information. Insights are useful pieces of information you didn't know, were reminded of, or were not currently using. They may include associate and customer motivations that you didn't recognize prior to interviews.

Do not use a recording device during interviews. They make some people uncomfortable and may limit what they're willing to share.

Think about what interviewees say, how their answers compare to what you already know, the potential value of their input and insights, and your own input and insights. Be sure to capture your thinking both during interviews and immediately afterward. An important benefit of the Process is that it disciplines and captures your thinking.

As you work through this step, you are doing two things: gathering information and thinking about it in a disciplined way that helps you focus on what your traditional and new customers need now. Capabilities and Communication can be difficult to separate because information, data, facts, research, etc. can fall into both categories. As such, placing thoughts/insights/inputs in both categories is fine.

The following descriptions of the information categories will help you decide which categories inputs and insights fit into:

A **Customer** is any person or entity your organization can create benefits for, including traditional customer types, potential customer types, and people who could influence customers.

Needs are business needs or personal needs, especially those that have changed in the last few years or are changing now.

Needs for business-to-business customers are the needs of businesses (i.e. fast delivery, quality, follow-up, new products, accurate invoicing).

Needs for consumer customers are the needs of consumers and the believed needs of the people who influence them.

Capabilities are all the things your organization has (or could have) to meet the needs of both old and new customers. They include: product features, services, good performance, endurance tests (either already done or scheduled), associate knowledge, software program features that help meet a customer's needs, research and development breakthroughs, manufacturing equipment or processes, manufacturing facilities, the skills of associates, and location advantages. They may be things you know about or things that have been forgotten or just not used or fully developed. Capabilities that pay off with traditional customers may need only slight adaptations to pay off with new customers. Be open-minded about capabilities. Think of them as anything that could help your organization meet current or new customer needs.

Communications – Information is information that associates or customers identify as useful to them, such as information on how products or services meet customer needs, statistics that show your organization's record of meeting customer needs, case histories, service performance levels, product features that meet customer needs, volume of work done by your products or services, quality of products and services, and their benefits.

Good customer experiences are part of "Communication – Information." They happen when your products or services benefit customers. On-time delivery, complete delivery, easy to follow assembly instructions, assistance getting full potential value, cost savings, affordable service, and positive responses to complaints are examples of good experiences. In future steps, you will learn how to generate good experiences and share them with customers.

Communications – Media is media and other communication techniques, such as associate attitudes and demeanor, conversations, presentations, what you and your associates do and say day after day, your recognition of associates' contributions, letters, emails, intranet messages, the goals and objectives of associates, advertising, publicity, point-of-sale materials, web advertising, websites, video, signs, and literature. Keep in mind that most of what you and your associates do and say is powerful communication (positive or negative), and will be your primary internal and external media whether you want it to be or not.

Benefits are the advantages you, your associates, and your products or services deliver or could deliver to customers. Benefits can be time savings, money savings, increased efficiency, reliability, follow-up communications, durability, style, or even just your willingness to keep customers informed. Benefits that cement a lasting differentiation between you and your competitors can be created by your associates when they know what customers need, even if competing products are similar.

With business customers, there are benefits for their organizations (such as increased efficiency) and benefits for their associates (such as delivery updates). Both are opportunities to distinguish your organization.

For consumer customers, there are factual benefits and emotional benefits. Increased gas mileage is a factual benefit. Automobile body styling and color are emotional benefits.

Consider the needs of both traditional and new customers as you document the benefits your organization delivers or could deliver.

Encourage interviewees to be broad-minded in their thinking about customers, needs, capabilities, communications, and benefits.

The following examples can help your associates and customers think with you. Share them when appropriate.

Examples of learning about customers and their needs

As a young man, I worked in marketing for Piper Aircraft Corporation. We identified our customers' needs in terms of the performance of our aircraft compared to competitive planes. One day, W. T. Piper, Sr., founder of the company, dropped by my office. He was in his eighties, and was board chairman. He asked me to show him how we marketed. I explained how we'd compared the performance of our aircraft to that of the competition.

He asked me why I worked there. I told him: "I love to fly." He told me that many of our customers bought our airplanes for the same reason and reminded me that they needed airplanes they could afford to buy and fly. The man who made the Piper Cub one of the world's most famous airplanes was right. Part of our job was to make flying affordable for people who love to fly. We needed to keep that in mind from design through production, marketing, and sales. It was part of our brand. Later, with the introduction of the turbine-powered Cheyenne, it was important to position this aircraft as a modern, high-tech airplane at the top of the Piper lineup.

During a summer vacation from college, I worked as an intern for a daily newspaper. I interviewed an elderly lady who'd operated a country store for many years and wrote a feature story about her. The story was full of descriptions of the old-fashioned candy counter, the barrels, and the shelves of merchandise that dated back decades. The feature editor read the story and sent me back to get more information. "Our readers need to know more than just what the typical country store looked like," he said. "They need new information, especially about people." During my second visit, I learned the lady had the first phone in Portersville, N.Y., a suburb of Buffalo. I asked her about the first time it rang. She said: "I answered it and a voice said 'quick, send the doctor, the President has been shot.'" The president was William McKinley. The date was 1901. I had a story about that tragedy that met our readers' need for new information because I finally asked the right questions.

I was interviewing the president of a worldwide engineering firm. He told me about a need he'd had and explained how he'd filled it, and that has helped me help many other managers. When I asked him about his associates and customers, he opened a drawer in his desk. "This is my feel-good drawer," he said. "I keep documents here from associates and customers that make me feel good." He read several to me. They were notes from associates and customers from across the world thanking him for noticing and complimenting their work and for his firm's help with their business. "Everyone needs to know when they do things right," he told me.

Thanking people for what they do helped him get results. It is an important part of the Process. As you thank people, be sure to mention some specifics about what they did and how it contributed to meeting customers' needs.

Flatbed trailer operators need to ensure increased safety, less damage to cargos, and lower maintenance costs. Through interviews, we learned to quantify the benefits of our client's unique trailer flooring in all three areas. In the past, the firm's marketing and sales were directed at trailer manufacturers. They were slow to adopt the innovations. So we took the benefits to trade shows attended by flatbed trailer operators. Reaching the operators directly and explaining how our product could benefit them created a pull-through effect. Today, thousands of trailers featuring our client's flooring ride our highways.

Traditional customers of a district attorney's office were crime victims. New customers identified in interviews were parents of juveniles who worried their children might be lured into criminal activity. These parents needed help educating their children about the dangers of involvement in crime and how to avoid it. The district attorney developed programs that helped parents equip youngsters with the knowledge they needed to resist peer pressure to commit crimes. The programs worked and were duplicated by other district attorneys.

Traditional customers of a law firm were physicians involved in malpractice lawsuits. Spouses and other family members of physicians coping with malpractice lawsuits were identified as new customers. They needed help seeing the suit as a part of modern business rather than as a personal attack. This need inspired these lawyers to take the time to explain cases to families. The additional service made the firm a leader in this type of defense work.

Traditional customers of a billiards table manufacturer were middle-aged men who played billiards. Interviews revealed that women were potential customers. Women interviewed pointed out their need for a family game in which all ages and both genders are equal (strength and size aren't advantages in billiards). Promotion of the brand's appeal to women and young players just learning the game sent sales climbing.

Examples of capabilities

Interviews at the billiards table manufacturer uncovered university research that showed the firm's tables were consistently more accurate than competitors' products. The research was a new capability we put to work building sales with new players, especially women. Accurate tables make all new players—women as well as men—enjoy the game more, because properly executed shots can send the balls into the pockets from any position on the table. The research, which had been all but forgotten in a file, helped drive up sales.

Interviews with associates in the customer service and shipping departments of a building supplies manufacturer provided insight into an existing but unused capability of the firm that could help meet their customers' need to know when materials would arrive at building sites. A feature of an existing software program was identified and put to work informing contractors of the date materials would be delivered. The new service built relationships with contractors that in turn generated repeat sales without additional selling expenses.

Examples of communication

Interviews with associates of a printing company that sells point-of-sale materials to gas stations and convenience stores revealed that showing their salespeople the firm's sales results for all team members and providing customers with tips on how to use point-of-sale would motivate sales associates and customers. Regular communication of sales updates—posted on a bulletin board—motivated sales associates to greater efforts. Hints for customers on how to use point-of-sale to increase retail sales were communicated by phone and motivated customers to buy. Sales soared.

Interviews with associates of a company that manufactures farm and landscape products quantified the number of acres their machines mowed each year. We built the number into promotions. The number (in millions of acres per year) told new customers that this firm was a leader in the industry and helped drive an expansion into new markets.

Interviews with business owners who lease office space combined with local research turned ordinary communication materials—a "for lease" sign and sales flyer—into powerful tools for an office building. Potential customers said convenience was a top priority. The number of restaurants, express package drop-offs, and interstate connections within a few miles were determined and advertised on the sign and in the sales flyer. The building leased out in record time.

Interviews with the owner, sales manager, and end-user customers of the firm that manufactured flooring for flatbed trailers quantified the number of areas susceptible to damage and rot that were protected by the company's product. Presented at trade shows through a simple brochure, this information showed how easily and economically these hazards could be reduced by our client's product. Our client became and remains the key source for this unique flooring in the United States.

Examples of Benefits

The benefit to the point-of-sale printing company was increased sales. The benefit to their customers was increased sales. The benefit to sales associates was more money in commissions.

The farm and landscape manufacturer's customers benefitted from products that stood up to heavy use in rugged environments and the savings in time and money these provided.

The benefits to trailer operators from the new trailer component were longer lasting, safer trailers and lower maintenance costs, plus less damage to cargoes.

One of the benefits to parents of our client's billiards tables was a way to keep their children entertained at home.

Interview yourself last. You will have your own answers to the questions. It is likely you will modify them or expand them as you learn what others think. You will see the connections between the different categories of information, which will help you gauge their practicality. Write notes about your answers and categorize them the same way you did with associates and customers.

Enjoy doing the interviews. I think of it as "gold MINDING" You are mining the nuggets of gold in the interviewees' minds and helping them articulate those nuggets and benefit from them.

Use the Step 2 worksheet in the Worksheets section at the back of this book to guide you through capturing important input and insights.

STEP 3

Analyze Interviews

In this step, you will review the selected information from Step 2, further refine it, add more of your own input, and select items as opportunities. This is the most difficult and important step, so take your time. The extra effort will pay off.

Information from different interviewees is often similar and interrelated. Grouping it by categories makes it easier to recognize similar input (and to get an indication of how important the information may be to associates and customers or how widespread a perception may be) as well as visualize the relationships between needs, capabilities, communications, benefits, and your input (i.e. capabilities can also be communications-information that can make customers aware of your organization's ability to deliver benefits they need).

At this step, your thinking is being combined with input from associates and customers. This combination rarely happens in marketing and business planning, so it places you a step ahead of your competitors. You form this combination as you choose the information from your interviews that will help you meet your customers' current needs to use as you move forward.

Be open-minded about customers, new customer types, needs, capabilities, communication (information and media), benefits, and your input.

Remember that the origin of the information used in the Process gives it special credibility. You're not just using your experiences and thinking or that of a management team or consultant; you're using information from the people on the front line—customers and the associates who contact them. It is also the input and thinking of associates and customers who are doing the work and who have learned what pays off and what doesn't. Explain this fact to your associates as you work through the Process and reference the information obtained in interviews when it is helpful.

Example of customer

Corporate recruiters are customers for the college we assisted. Recruiters, combined with the education and career services provided by the college, help students get jobs when they graduate. By learning and meeting recruiters' needs, the college attracts recruiters from more businesses and expands employment opportunities for graduating students.

Example of new customer need

Academic training is the traditional need of college students. We learned from interviews that students had another important need the college could fill: non-academic experiences for students and instruction in how to effectively describe these experiences on resumes and in job interviews. Providing experience opportunities and helping students understand and present the value of their experiences to future employers became a new way of meeting students' needs while they were in school and when they graduated.

Example of new application of existing capability

Identifying and constructing the tough features that farmers and landscape contractors know help products last for years paid off for our farm and landscape products manufacturer year after year. We adapted this capability to similar needs of another customer segment: people who move to the country for the lifestyle but don't take up farming as their full-time vocation. While some products for these groups are different, both groups need tough products because they work a long way from services, and work stoppages can be expensive. Building robust features into the new products and promoting them to the new customers paid off with this new customer segment. These new customers valued the good things they heard from professional farmers about our client's durable products.

Example of communication – information

The district attorney we worked with is an expert in personal communications. He pays attention to how his associates meet the needs of their customers and then reminds them of their service as he thanks them in individual conversations. This recognition inspires them further and motivates other associates. We helped him describe the process in the first chapter of Managing Prosecutors, *a management text published by the National College of District Attorneys.*

Example of communication – media

We helped the district attorney communicate the benefits of internal communications to other district attorneys through national media.

Example of a new benefit

A new and important benefit a municipal botanical garden could deliver to their customers was identified from input in interviews. The botanical garden is now "growing" people by providing useful information to them, such as the identities of plants that thrive in the local environment, and by spotlighting new potential hobbies or careers in horticulture. By combining plants with enthusiastic volunteers who provided learning experiences for adults and children, the gardens enriched the lives of visitors and built attendance.

Take your time with this step and seek input from your associates. At this point, you are documenting information you will use to build sales and brand value year after year. Short of the associate and customer interviews, this is the most important step in the Process because it is here that you recognize the valuable input and insights that will be your keys to building sales and brand value without spending a fortune on marketing, advertising, and branding.

Use the Step 3 worksheet in the Worksheets section at the back of this book to analyze your inputs and insights.

STEP 4

Identify Brand Benefit

Your Brand Benefit focuses everything you and your associates do to effectively and efficiently meet the current needs of customers and new customer types.

Your Brand Benefit is vital because it links everything your organization does—including what associates do or say, product and service development, sales, customer relations, manufacturing, advertising, website content, service, delivery, marketing, warranty service, finance, billing and more—to the fulfillment of your customers' needs.

Your Brand Benefit:

- Focuses all associates on meeting customer needs
- Is the key to presenting one compelling promise and graphic presentation of how you meet customers' needs
- Helps you and your associates use every capability and every communication method (information as well as media) to promise and deliver what your customers need… and get credit for it

- Guides you in growing sales and building a powerful brand simultaneously.

Your Brand Benefit will also help your organization do the things that pay off and avoid those that don't. Its effectiveness will spread throughout the organization because it will be used to develop your Compelling Focus and your Brand Promise, the cornerstones of effective internal and external communications.

Examples of Brand Benefits:

For a residential development, we created a Brand Benefit for homebuilders who could buy lots to build on and another for homebuyers who could buy homes as they were being constructed. For builders, the Brand Benefit was a comprehensive plan to sell homes in this neighborhood more quickly and at better prices than homes in other neighborhoods. That meant homebuilders were safer building speculative homes there. For homebuyers, the Brand Benefits came from receiving what they needed in their new homes, neighborhood, and location. They got more of what they needed and were more likely to be able to resell their homes at good prices.

The Brand Benefit of the farm and landscape products manufacturer was durability and reliability. It was more than just words—it was the fact that the firm always delivered these things. It was the integrity of the firm's associates and the resulting long-term performance of its products combined.

The Brand Benefit for the botanical gardens we worked with was the knowledge and excitement students, families, homeowners, and other visitors gained from the plants and from the volunteers who made the plants useful to visitors' lives. The volunteers provided information on plants that would flourish in visitors' homes and yards, along with environmental information that increased their appreciation of nature and, in some cases, inspired students to study science.

The Brand Benefit of the district attorney's office we worked with was increased safety for all citizens by prosecuting crime faster and more effectively while also preventing crimes before they took place. This was achieved by interrupting the processes that lead young people into crime.

Arrive at your Brand Benefit by reviewing the customers, customer needs, capabilities, communications, and benefits you selected for the Information Analysis Chart in the Step 3 worksheet. Then write drafts of your Brand Benefit by summarizing the benefits your organization will deliver to its customers. It may help to write drafts from the perspectives of your different customer types and then create a version broad enough to appeal to all of them. Don't try to make them cute. Just capture the benefits your associates, products, and services can deliver to customers now (or could later, after some changes or additions).

Next, edit your drafts and create your final version. Once you have your final version, go through it and underline the information that came from associate and customer input. This step will show you how well you are utilizing input from associates and customers.

Use the Step 4 worksheet in the Worksheets section at the back of this book to identify your Brand Benefit

STEP 5

Define Your Compelling Focus

In this step, you transform your Brand Benefit into a unique mission statement that is a clear definition of how you and your associates behave to profitably meet customers' needs.

Mission statements are frequently watered down by compromises until they offer little or no definition of how associates deliver the Brand Benefit. They are watered down because they are created with little or no input from associates and customers and do not define behavior that serves customer needs. They may be the result of too many compromises among managers.

Some mission statements promise that organizations will "operate with integrity and respect for others." Customers find little that is unique in that. Few customers will consider buying from a company if they don't believe its associates operate with integrity and respect for others; these are givens with customers. Without them, no Brand Benefit is going to be consistently delivered. No relationship is going to work for long.

Using such broad concepts in your mission statement won't distinguish your organization from your competitors. They sound nice, but they don't provide your associates with specific guidance on how to behave as they meet customers' current needs.

The Compelling Focus is specific. It defines how you and the people of your organization behave to deliver your organization's Brand Benefit. It guides the many decisions you and your associates make daily.

Defining how associates should behave to deliver your Brand Benefit is so much more effective than using generalized mission statements that I gave it a special name: the Compelling Focus. The name reminds you and your associates that your focus must be compelling for both associates and customers. This Compelling Focus guides you and your associates' decisions, actions, attitudes, and ideas. Associates follow it because it helps them serve customers and because they see you using it.

The Compelling Focus also provides guidance for customers. It tells customers what to expect from the people of your organization.

Your Compelling Focus should begin with the words "The people of (your organization's name)..." Then it should explain how you and the people in your organization deliver your Brand Benefit to customers. This beginning is important. It demonstrates that your organization's management understands that the Brand Benefit is created and delivered by the actions and attitudes of all associates, not just by products and services or the actions of one or a few associates. The similarity to the beginning of the Declaration of Independence isn't accidental. Both acknowledge that power comes from people.

The Compelling Focus forms an essential connection in the Process between what customers need and what you and your associates deliver. It is created from your organization's Brand Benefit and is unique to your organization because it is based on input and insights from you, your associates, and your customers. It focuses associates' thinking, actions, and attitudes on meeting current customer needs. It is your associates' guide to making your Brand Benefit a reality for customers. It creates for your organization the tremendous power of satisfied customers who will buy from you again and tell others about your products or services. It will help create a "buzz" that will be your most effective (as well as free) media.

How you apply your Compelling Focus will determine how effectively you and your associates create the difference between your organization and your competitors. Even if your products or services are similar to those offered by competitors, you can differentiate your organization through the quality and consistency of customer contacts and by highlighting the delivery of your Brand Benefit. Creating and using your Compelling Focus is an opportunity to make sure your organization meets the needs of both traditional and new customers alike.

Use the examples below (taken from my own experiences) to understand how other organizations use their Compelling Focus to define the associate behaviors that meet their customers' current needs by delivering their Brand Benefit. Move your Brand Benefit in the Step 4 worksheet to this worksheet and write drafts of your organization's Compelling Focus. In your drafts, define how associates use your selected capabilities and communications to deliver your Brand Benefit.

Don't discard drafts of your Compelling Focus as you write new ones. Borrow from them. Test them to make sure the behavior they describe meets customers' needs. Write and re-write.

The process of writing and re-writing helps you think and capture your thinking. It also helps you examine your work critically and strive to improve it.

Once you have a good draft of your Compelling Focus, share it with associates who are involved in the Process. Don't ask them if they like it; ask them how well it defines associate behavior that will meet customer needs and deliver your Brand Benefit. Consider their input.

Examples of Compelling Focus

The botanical garden's Brand Benefit is a special, safe environmental experience for people of all ages, education, and experience. It allows them to better understand their natural environment, preserve it, benefit from it, and tell others about it. The garden's Compelling Focus says: "The people of the Mobile Botanical Gardens provide experiences for visitors of all ages that help them appreciate and benefit from our unique environment."

The residential development's Brand Benefit for builder customers was a comprehensive plan to sell homes in the subdivision faster and at better prices than other neighborhoods. For homebuyer customers, the benefits resided in the quality of the homes, neighborhood, location, and the high resale value. The development's Compelling Focus said: "The people of the development company, real estate agents, designers, landscapers, and builders create and demonstrate the unique ways in which these new homes, this neighborhood, and this location provide homeowners with more of the benefits available in this unique area."

The Brand Benefit of the district attorney's office was their promise to serve every citizen in their jurisdiction rather than just those involved in the criminal justice system through faster, more efficient prosecution and measures that stop crimes before they happen. The district attorney's Compelling Focus said: "The people of the district attorney's office provide fair and vigorous prosecution under the law while supporting victims and witnesses; working to prevent crime before it happens; working with partners in ways that make them more effective; and communicating our role to partners, media, and the public."

Profitability is the lifeblood of American business. Consistent profitability comes from concentrating on doing the right things, not giving things away to make up for mistakes. The Compelling Focus contributes to profitability by guiding associates as they reach hundreds of decisions and take hundreds of actions to meet customer needs efficiently and effectively. It is the opposite of throwing things at unhappy customers to placate them. The mistakes it prevents and the customer relations it builds save valuable time and money and end paralyzing debates. Equipped with the Compelling Focus, associates can cut unproductive costs and change unproductive behavior as they increase quality, build sales, and grow brand value.

Use the Step 5 worksheet in the Worksheets section at the back of this book to prepare your Compelling Focus.

STEP 6

Create Your Brand Promise

Your Brand Promise is a short statement that promises your Brand Benefit. It sets up opportunities for your organization to differentiate itself by promising and proving that it can and does deliver what customers need.

In this step, you'll create a Brand Promise that summarizes your Brand Benefit in a few words; lasts a long time; and is more effective than a tagline, theme, or slogan.

Taglines, themes, and slogans are widely used in marketing and advertising. Many are empty promises that change with marketing materials, advertising campaigns, individual ads, literature, etc. Your Brand Promise will be much more than a tagline, theme, or slogan that changes before customers learn to recognize it.

Your Brand Promise is a promise you keep. It becomes more and more effective every time it is kept, especially when you point out to customers the good customer experiences that come with your products, services, or brand. In fact, keeping your Brand Promise is what will make your organization stand out from competitors in customers' minds, and this distinction will only strengthen as their good experiences with your organization mount up.

Presenting your Brand Benefit as a promise rather than a temporary tagline, theme, or slogan creates three advantages:

1. Expectation – customers expect you to keep a promise
2. Attitude – you and your associates intend to keep that promise
3. Action – you and your associates know and take the actions to ensure the promise is kept

Expectation, attitude, and action are all opportunities to show that your organization meets customers' needs better than your competitors.

Your Brand Promise should be as short as possible. This is important because you will use your Brand Promise in almost all communications materials, from signs to letterhead to advertising to sales conversations. The amount of space required to present it in type large enough to be easily read varies between different communication materials (more space is available on your website than on your business card), but space is always limited.

Use a verb if it works, but don't use a verb just for the sake of using one. Be broad so your Brand Promise can easily apply to future products and services.

Examples of Brand Promise

"Performance You Can Count On"™ *(trademark for Bush Hog®)) is the Brand Promise we created for a farm and landscape products manufacturer. Created years ago, it is still used to promise the reliability the company delivers worldwide.*

"The Cradle of the NFL" (Senior Bowl, Mobile Arts and Sports Association) is the Brand Promise developed for this unique national football bowl game where college football standouts showcase their talents to NFL coaches and scouts as well as stadium and television audiences. It summarizes the benefit of the bowl game to spectators, the television audience, the players, and the NFL. It was effective for years.

Taglines, themes, and slogans that change frequently are unproductive. Changes mean costs for new materials, but these costs are only the smallest fraction of their real cost. The real cost of changing taglines, themes, and slogans is the abandonment of whatever identity has already been built with associates and customers. You'll have to start over again to build a new one.

Your Brand Promise is for long-term use. Use it as long as it communicates your Brand Benefit. It should be used as an integral part of the brand logo in promotional materials including advertising, websites, literature, videos, point-of-sale communications, and even letterheads.

Your logo is a graphic representation of your brand. Skilled graphic designers can create simple logos that illustrate your Brand Promise. Your designer should review your Brand Benefit, your Brand Promise, and the environment your products or services are used in and then use his/her training, resources, and talents to create or update your logo for use with your Brand Promise in a form that—with consistent, frequent exposure—becomes immediately recognized by customers. Simple will work better than complicated. Test samples by seeing how recognizable they are at a distance. Remember: you are seeking to ensure instant recognition.

An immediately recognized logo that is consistent with your Brand Promise is superior to just any image or jumble of stylized letters because it makes it easier for customers to relate to your organization. Customers are more likely to say to themselves and others: "Buy the one with the bear image . . . it's strong."

Consistent use of the Brand Promise with the logo makes the logo more effective. Just a glance at a well-executed logo supported by a Brand Promise in a television spot or on a point-of-sale sign or a billboard can bring your products or services and their Brand Benefit to your customers' minds.

Logos do need to be updated occasionally. Images can become outdated or older images may be difficult to reproduce in modern media, or your logo may have been created without proper consideration of all the ways it could be used. Maybe it only works in four-color applications. Update the logo without destroying it by making subtle changes. Make sure you involve associates, especially sales associates and distribution professionals, as they will have to explain the changes to customers.

The speed at which customers recognize your logo and Brand Promise is important because television and computer screens present information quickly. Television and computer screens use the power of motion to draw and hold the eye. You have probably noticed how your eyes are drawn to television and computer screens even when you aren't looking for them. It's because motion is easily detected by the eyes and draws attention. Effective logos can be designed to take advantage of motion as they appear on the screen. Brand Promises can appear as if they are being written across the screen by an invisible hand.

Of course, television and computer screens are not the only applications of your logo and Brand Promise. Consider how they will work together in all possible applications, those you use today and those you may use in the future. Check how they'll work by doing practical things: put your prospective logo on a large application such as a sign and see for yourself how far away you can be and still read it. Put it on a small application such as a business card and make sure you recognize the image and can read the Brand Promise as well as the other information. Be sure your logo will work in black and white, two-color, and four-color applications.

Keep in mind that your Brand Benefit should drive the artwork of your logo and Brand Promise. The artwork is the visual execution of the Brand Benefit, not the driver. Artwork can be seductive. Don't let logo design bury your Brand Benefit—you are not selling the logo design. Ask yourself and your associates how well the artwork communicates your Brand Benefit.

Logos are sometimes used by themselves in non-promotional applications such as corporate papers. That means your organization's logo must work with the Brand Promise and by itself.

The words of your Brand Promise should be bold enough to stimulate thinking, questions, and even a challenge from customers. A natural reaction of customers to a promise is to ask for proof that your organization will keep it. They ask: "How do you do that?" That's just what you want. It's an opening—provided by your customers and prospects—to present specific reasons you will keep your Brand Promise. It's your invitation to sell. In the next step, you will learn how to respond to this challenge and make your Brand Promise even more effective.

Taglines, slogans and themes used in commerce are often written to be cute. Cute is supposed to grab attention. Cute taglines, slogans, and themes can be examples of "undisciplined creativity." They sound good by themselves and may even be humorous, but they can become liabilities as customers compare their experiences to their expectations. They may even snicker at a tagline or advertisement because it doesn't describe their own experience.

"Disciplined creativity" is creativity that maintains the connection between the Brand Benefit, the Brand Promise, and the act of keeping that promise. It is more specific than "undisciplined creativity," which may not be connected to anything you do to meet customer needs. "Disciplined creativity" pays off because your organization builds a reputation for making its Brand Promise come true for customers.

Taglines, themes, and slogans developed with "undisciplined creativity," as well as the advertising and marketing materials that use them, may promote something that isn't delivered. "Undisciplined creativity" doesn't accomplish much except entertain the people who write it and sometimes those who approve it. Laughing isn't the same as buying; it doesn't build a connection between customer needs and what the organization delivers. It can be frustrating and even embarrassing for salespeople.

Don't be distracted by "undisciplined creativity" or distract your customers with it. Put "disciplined creativity" to work to create a bold, compelling logo and Brand Promise combination that says you deliver a benefit your customers need. Insist that your logo and Brand Promise designs be part of your Process. Use your logo and Brand Promise consistently. Make it clear to your associates, distributors, and vendors how your logo and Brand Promise must appear in all applications.

Example of undisciplined creativity in advertising

The marketing staff and advertising agency for a healthcare organization that was losing customers proudly showed me their television advertising based on a cute slogan and logo. They laughed at the funny slice-of-life skits depicted on the screen. So did I. But the laughter died when I asked them how the advertising promised what their customers said they needed: the best healthcare.

Read your Brand Benefit out loud and use it as a guide as you write your Brand Promise. Don't try to be cute. Write down your thoughts. Write many drafts. Writing will stimulate your thinking. Keep referring back to your Brand Benefit to stay on track. If the statements get long, edit them. Take your time. Stop after you have captured all your thoughts in one sitting. Take a break. Sleep on it. Let your mind work on it while you are relaxing. Effective Brand Promises have been conceived in a shower or on a walk. Keep pen and paper handy to catch your thoughts. Allow your subconscious to work. Then go back to writing.

Keep in mind that you are writing a promise. It will be more effective than a tagline, theme, or slogan because it is a promise. It will become more and more effective as your organization keeps it and tells customers about it.

Write your Brand Promise in the form of a promise by saying "We promise" to yourself as you write. Make your Brand Promise broad enough to encompass your Brand Benefit as it applies to traditional and new customers.

Example of Brand Promises

The Brand Promise we created for the residential development in an area known for its beautiful waterfront and excellent schools as well as outstanding health, recreational, and retail facilities is: "Everything You Love about the Eastern Shore." It promised that all the benefits of this area were at the fingertips of homeowners in the development. It solicited this challenge from customers: "Show me!" Proof was already prepared and provided in advertising, brochure copy, and point outlines for sales conversations. They included names of the schools, health, recreational, and retail facilities within a short distance of the subdivision (the distance to each was also provided). The copywriter and artist who created the advertising and brochure used "disciplined creativity" to bring the benefits of the attractions and their accessibility alive in words, photos, and illustrations.

Don't throw away an existing tagline, slogan or theme your organization may already use. If it communicates your Brand Benefit, you may be able to improve it by writing it as a promise and ensuring that it is meaningful to all your customers, old and new alike.

Use the Step 6 worksheet in the Worksheets section at the back of this book to prepare your Brand Promise.

STEP 7

Define Your Brand Proof

Now you are ready to make your Brand Promise effective with different types of customers by identifying and presenting Brand Proof that makes it clear that your Brand Benefit will pay off for them.

You do this by selecting and converting the capabilities and communications you selected in the Step 3 worksheet into examples and information that prove your organization's products or services keep your Brand Promise with different types of customers. Brand Proof is the key to generating more buying action with more than one type of traditional customer because it illustrates how your products or services meet their specific needs. The more specific your Brand Proof, the more effective it is.

Brand Proof works in four ways:

- It makes products or services and their benefits relevant to different types of customers
- It builds the value of the Brand Promise

- It answers the question your Brand Promise elicits from customers ("will it work for me?") with specific information that is relevant to their needs
- It does what salespeople often find themselves trying to do alone—connects advertising and marketing with sales

Brand Proof is developed from your selected capabilities and communications. Capabilities and communications expressed as proof that your products or services deliver on your Brand Promise for specific types of customers make your promise more effective; the proof backs up the promise with information that is meaningful to specific types of customers.

Brand Proof can refer to capabilities or communications you already have and are using, as well as materials/capabilities you could use differently or modify. I have learned them from interviews with associates, customers, engineers, field salespeople, customer service people, and distributors.

Brand Proof is factual and should be presented in the form of hard facts, not as superlatives or generalities. It takes information out of the realm of advertising, where customers believe you can say anything you want, and moves it into the realm of reliable information. It meets your customers' need for reliable information in a world of hype and half-truths. It works with your Brand Promise by proving you will keep it.

Capabilities and communications that can be Brand Proof may include: product features, services, performance tests, durability tests, case histories, the amount of work performed by products over a year, services and their benefits for customers, location advantages, customer experiences, fast service parts fulfillment speed, and processes that make it easy to do business with your organization. Follow up to make sure customers are satisfied. Other capabilities or information you may already have (or could have) that show different types of customers that your products or services deliver your Brand Promise can also be Brand Proof.

If you are familiar with communication strategies and techniques, you may at first confuse Brand Proof with "messaging" (information organizations want to deliver to their customers). There is an important difference. Brand Proof illustrates the payoff of your Brand Promise for different types of customers, including new customers. It consists of specific illustrations of how your Brand Promise meets a specific type of customer's needs. It makes your Brand Promise relevant to different customer types, builds your sales argument, and adds to the credibility of your Brand Promise. Standard messages used by some marketers aren't as effective as Brand Proof because they don't prove the efficacy of a Brand Promise developed from a Brand Benefit sourced from customers' and associates' needs.

Your Brand Promise should be as prominent internally as it is externally. It is a promise from all associates to meet customers' needs.

It works with all associates and customers by promising to meet an overall need identified by customers. It is presented in the same words to all customers and associates. It is a single, unchanging promise that comes with everything your firm provides. It is made relevant to individual customers, whether new or old, with Brand Proof.

While the Brand Promise may remain unchanged for years, new Brand Proof should be constantly researched and developed. With specific customer types, you may use Brand Proof as the lead aspect of your marketing and sales materials, but you should always include your logo and Brand Promise. Likewise, it is important to relate specific Brand Proof to your Brand Promise in sales conversations and copy so as to pave the way for the sale of other products or services.

Illustration of Brand Promise and Brand Proof

I use the analogy of a mason building a strong brick wall to illustrate how properly prepared Brand Proof is effective in itself and contributes to the effectiveness of the Brand Promise. The wall represents the Brand Promise. Each brick represents Brand Proof. As masons build a brick wall, they choose the bricks carefully, discarding those that are broken. Each brick chosen provides its own strength and contributes to the overall strength of the wall. The Brand Proof bricks in your Brand Promise wall are capabilities and communications that prove your organization keeps its promise in ways that are important to different types of customers, including new customers. The successful performance of your products/services and associates becomes additional proof in your customers' minds.

Steps taken to grow your organization—new facilities, new services, improved products—are also Brand Proof. But don't just brag about growth when you use them; instead, explain how new facilities, new services, and improved products help your organization deliver on its Brand Promise. Do the same with important business decisions as they are announced to shareholders, associates, and customers.

Example of the Brand Promise/Brand Proof relationship

All the plants and learning experiences available at the botanical garden are proof it will deliver on its Brand Promise of "Come Here to Grow." When the gardens asked an architectural firm to create a new garden design, it was important that the architects, the board of directors, employees, volunteers, and the public viewed the new design as additional Brand Proof. The garden was getting better at delivering growing experiences for people, not launching a new mission for the gardens themselves. Explaining it this way helped keep the garden's associates and members focused on communicating one clear Brand Promise through everything they did. The new design became additional proof that the gardens would keep their promise.

Example of a Brand Proof selling products while supporting a Brand Promise

Farmers know farm machinery and its components. They know that quality bearings are important. Pointing out again and again the quality bearings (or other tough features) used in our client's farm equipment was proof that the firm's Brand Promise of durability was a reality for all its products.

View new developments, new processes, new equipment, and new products and services as Brand Proof that supports your Brand Promise. Explain how these additions support the Brand Promise as they are introduced. New products and their features, for example, should be introduced in terms of how they help your organization keep its Brand Promise. This will ensure these new products take advantage of the reputation of the Brand Promise and enhance it.

Example of a Brand Proof used to sell a new product and validate a Brand Promise

When we introduced new products for the farm and landscape equipment manufacturer, we highlighted their rugged features as proof of their durability. Because of this approach, the new product itself (as well as the publicity, literature, and advertising used in its introduction) proved that the company had delivered on the firm's Brand Promise of durability. The new product introduction worked for the brand and contributed to it. This consistency in communications created a multi-million-dollar brand and consistent sales increases with small budgets compared to competitors.

Repetition pays off in marketing and sales. It especially pays off when the focus is on presenting more and more examples of Brand Proof rather than the same proof over and over. New Brand Proof captures attention, influences customers in different ways, and influences different types of customers. Consistency is retained because the new Brand Proof still supports the same Brand Promise. Today, electronic communications make it easy and economical to communicate new Brand Proof to customers through websites, social media, and other digital marketing methods. Regularly updating Brand Proof is an effective way to bring visitors back to your website again and again as they find new information. Constantly develop new Brand Proof and communicate it in your marketing, advertising, and sales to your associates and customers.

A successful brand is a promise that is made, proven, and kept. The combination of Brand Promise and Brand Proof gets attention and delivers good reasons to buy specific products or services, which in turn reflects well on all your products and services. Don't forget to include good customer experiences in your collection of Brand Proof.

You may need to change the wording of capabilities or communications so they make sense as proof. Often that means presenting them in as few words as possible so that customers can scan them quickly. It is effective to use bullets points when mentioning capabilities or communications in copy.

Examples of the effectiveness of Brand Proof

Over more than thirty years, we helped build one of the world's most powerful brands in its field. This was accomplished by consistently presenting the company's Brand Promise and developing solid Brand Proof that showed their products, services, and associates kept that Promise. The brand was built while competing with the largest firm in the industry.

During an interview, a customer service rep at the company that made billiards tables described university research that showed their tables were more accurate than their competitors' products. The research was "Communications – Information" that had never been used with customers. We used it to show that a properly executed shot on this manufacturer's tables would go in the pocket more consistently than on tables from other manufacturers. That meant new players as well as experienced players would have more fun with this brand. The Brand Promise of more fun backed up by the Brand Proof the tables delivered drove a huge sales increase.

An engineer at a client firm told me that traction tests would show his company's utility vehicles had more pulling power than competitors' machines. Tests pulling a weight transfer sled were videotaped with his company's product set against competitors' products. Our client's competitors' machines spun out after a few feet. Our client's product pulled the weight transfer sled to the end of the track. We used the gap in the distance between how far our client's product pulled the weight and how far the competitors' machines pulled it as Brand Proof of superior performance. Sales went up.

Engineers at a famous boat manufacturer showed me how material between the interior and exterior of their hulls expanded to make their hulls a solid structure and the boats unsinkable. Based on this feature, we created the Thump Test, a quick, easy way customers could prove to themselves that our client's boats were superior. It was promoted with a sign on the hull that invited boat show visitors to "Thump here." In this way, customers would hear the thump of a solid hull and compare it to the rattle of competitive boats. The test was used to introduce a new model and helped sell out production in just a few weeks.

Review the capabilities and communications you selected on your Information Analysis Chart for information that can become Brand Proof. Ask your marketing, sales, engineering, and service associates for examples of product features and services and think about how they deliver on your Brand Promise. Write them as facts. Make them short enough to be used as bullets in copy.

Use the Step 7 worksheet in the Worksheets section at the back of this book to prepare your Brand Proof.

STEP 8

Ask the Compelling Focus Question

The Compelling Focus Question is the question you and your associates ask and answer to make sure all decisions are made with due consideration of your Compelling Focus.

In this step, you and your associates pledge to ask how their decisions match with the behaviors defined in your Compelling Focus. This brings the Compelling Focus into the thinking of associates and helps them make choices that build sales and brand value. It may be as simple as being patient with an unhappy customer. The answer and the results for customers or other associates should be captured and shared with other associates so they are encouraged to use the question as they make decisions. Recognition of those who use the question will motivate others to use it. Form 12 G in the materials for Step 12 is used to report examples of applying the Compelling Focus Question, the answer and the results achieved. This step can be applied when making decisions about strategy, tactics, attitudes, new products or services, product features, manufacturing, marketing, sales, finance, shipping, delivery, cost reduction, purchases, and more.

Every decision you and your associates make can support, break, or ignore your Compelling Focus. Step 8 helps you and your associates ask yourselves how a decision fits into your Compelling Focus or, if it doesn't, why it doesn't. It ensures decisions—small as well as big—are consistent with your organization's commitment to meeting customers' current needs.

Many organizations value managers' decisions while not fully recognizing the value of decisions made by other associates. They miss the value of most decision-making. Associates, especially those who deal with customers and new products, make far more decisions that affect an organization's success than managers. Associates' decisions, attitudes, the actions they take or do not take, and how well they perform influence other associates and customers.

A customer service representative's attitude of concern conveyed to a frustrated customer, a sales representative taking the time to look up a specification for a customer, a customer service rep proactively calling a customer about a shipping delay, a manager deciding not to buy a new software program that cuts costs by curbing customer service, a marketing manager rejecting the promotion of a benefit the organization doesn't deliver . . . all are examples of important decisions that affect the futures of organizations. Decisions like these take place in organizations of every size, from a single-person sales representative firm to a multi-national corporation. The ability to make the right decisions is the backbone of a powerful brand. Making the wrong decisions chips away at that spine.

Implementation is where the rubber meets the road in businesses, professions, government, and non-profit organizations. Implementing decisions made by associates controls the outcome of strategic decisions made by managers. Decisions made by associates represent your products or services and brand far more effectively (for good or bad) than advertising and promotion. Yet few organizations provide associates with practical guidance on how to make the right decisions.

Many tools help guide decision-making today. Spreadsheet analysis is frequently used because it makes it easy to do "what ifs".

The instant calculations and charts are convenient and impressive. But they can lead to decisions that de-motivate associates and push away customers. Users tend to focus on the numerical results without paying enough attention to what is behind the numbers. Without consideration of the human elements, a spreadsheet-only-guided decision can damage your business's relationship with associates and customers.

You and your associates will make the right decisions by asking yourselves, "How does my decision about this match our Compelling Focus?" It is simple, direct, and effective. Asking and answering it requires thinking about and applying the Compelling Focus. It is an opportunity to understand how a decision supports or undermines it. It is a simple way to ensure all associates are able to make their decisions contribute to the Process. The question taps into the wealth of experience and knowledge of associates and makes sure they think about and focus on meeting customer needs.

Asking and answering the Compelling Focus Question leads to decisions that may be as simple as looking up a specification for a customer or prospect, advising a customer of a shipping delay in time for them to change their schedule, saying "Whoa" when something doesn't look right on the production line, choosing a software program that cuts costs without curbing service, and not promoting a benefit that isn't delivered.

The Compelling Focus Question contributes to decisions that save costs and improve efficiency. It stimulates creative thinking by managers and associates that preserves value while cutting costs or increasing efficiency. It works because it makes thinking about serving customers a part of decision-making.

This doesn't mean numbers and spreadsheets aren't useful. They can help control costs and make decisions. But spreadsheets don't take into account human motivations and perceptions. They don't consider customer needs. That still has to be done by human thinking. The Compelling Focus Question helps guide that thinking.

The Compelling Focus Question is a powerful link in the Process, especially when it is used by everyone. After a while, it becomes instinctive. When management uses it in decision-making and explains the relationship of decisions to the Compelling Focus, it signals to every associate that they take the Compelling Focus seriously. Every decision associates make with the guidance of the Compelling Focus Question encourages other associates to use it. As management recognizes associates for using the Compelling Focus Question, more associates will use it.

The Compelling Focus Question helps make the attitudes and actions of all associates a powerful, credible media that builds your brand internally and externally. And it costs nothing. In a business environment where standardized business practices and technologies are making many products and services the same, the Compelling Focus Question and the thinking and actions it elicits from you and your associates can make your products, services, and brand stand out. It can also increase your organization's efficiency by focusing everyone on making decisions that benefit your customers as well as your organization.

Examples of the Compelling Focus Question paying off

Associates asking the Compelling Focus Question can prevent serious missteps. Associates of a savings bank we worked with refused to implement the decision of a new vice president. The new executive didn't think the bank's long-standing reputation for paying compound interest on CDs was important to its associates and customers. Compound interest, the great benefit of interest paid on interest, was a benefit the bank's associates had provided to savers for years. Customers knew its value. But the new vice president didn't believe they would notice if it was stopped. Internally, he touted the potential interest savings of the bank. When he insisted associates sell CDs without compound interest, they appealed his order to the bank's president. The president asked the

Compelling Focus Question and then reversed the decision before it could undo years of brand-building.

An associate of a another bank we worked with (located on the island of Oahu in Hawaii) used the Compelling Focus Question when she asked herself how she could fulfill the bank's commitment to meet customers' needs through superior service as she finished up mortgage loan documents for a customer who lived on a nearby island. Standard procedure was to mail the paperwork to the customer for her signature—a process that could take a week or more. The associate remembered that the customer was an inter-island airline pilot. She met her in the pilot's lounge when she landed in Honolulu the next day and got her signatures, speeding up the process by at least a week and making a lasting impression on a customer who met hundreds of potential bank customers every week.

An associate of a bank we worked with in the Southeast asked herself the Compelling Focus Question when she drove by an ATM on a Saturday and saw that the site was covered by overgrown grass and shrubs. She got the family lawnmower and clippers and made the ATM site attractive and safer for the bank's customers. When we told the bank's associates what she did, they imitated her behavior in a variety of positive ways.

Ask and answer the Compelling Focus Question and encourage your associates to ask and answer it. Request that recommendations you receive be accompanied by a review of how the request matches your organization's Compelling Focus. Set an example by asking the question of associates as they make requests.

Use the Step 8 worksheet in the Worksheets section at the back of this book to document examples of you and your associates asking the Compelling Focus Question and the positive actions that resulted.

STEP 9

Build Repeat Sales and Referrals

The power of good customer experiences with your products, services, and associates will build your brand and will generate repeat sales and referrals when you point out these good experiences to customers and ask for more business at the same time.

Repeat sales and referrals are special sales opportunities. They not only produce sales, but also reduce marketing, advertising, and sales costs by keeping existing customers loyal.

Step 9 shows you how to identify good customer experiences and communicate them to customers with requests for repeat sales or referrals. Good experiences can be as immediate as progress on the delivery of products or services or as long-range as instructions for customers on how they can garner benefits from your products or services over several years. Explain how good experiences are the fulfillment of your Brand Promise as you communicate them.

Repeat sales and referrals come from communicating good customer experiences. Good customer experiences come from associates knowing what customers need today, delivering it, and telling them how they delivered it.

Every part of the Process is important in providing customers with good experiences, but no matter how good you are at delivering good experiences, you still need to tell customers when they're experiencing them and ask for additional sales or referrals at the appropriate time. In this step, you'll identify your organization's opportunities to call good experiences to the attention of your customers and ask them to buy again or give you referrals.

Examples of communication techniques for telling customers about good experiences

In our practice, I wanted to be sure our clients knew how to use the materials we produced and be able to ask for additional business and referrals. As we completed components of their programs, such as brochures and product videos, I made a point of reviewing with our clients how to use the materials. As I did, clients saw their Brand Promise and Brand Proof at work. At the same time, I asked for additional work. Pleased with what they were experiencing and my interest in helping them, they frequently gave us new assignments.

A key communications method for a homebuilder we worked with for many years was showcasing homes under construction to customers at the framing stage, when they were completed, and a month after closing. These showcases showed customers the benefits they were receiving. The inspection after the sale reminded customers of the firm's warranty and after-sale service, and was another good experience. The demonstrations and inspection included requests for referrals. The firm received as much as 50 percent of its sales from referrals, saving thousands of dollars that weren't spent on advertising.

In today's world of compromises on everything from the words we use to the behaviors we permit, expectations aren't very high. You can get a feeling for this by visiting someone who did the contracting for their new home themselves. They will likely tell you about deliveries made in the afternoon that were scheduled for the morning when the work crew was there, or worse.

By combining your Brand Promise and Brand Proof, you can spread awareness that you promise to meet your customers' needs in all your communications.

Telling your customers that you are delivering or have delivered on your promise pays off and results in more satisfied customers and, in turn, more customers. Many organizations don't do it because they aren't sure they can always deliver what they promise. You eliminate this fear with the application of your company's Compelling Focus.

In Step 12, you will help associates consistently plan the right actions, take them, and receive recognition for taking them.

Whether you tell your customers you delivered on your promise or not, they already know it. If your firm's delivery is disappointing, customers are already talking about it and you aren't likely to keep their business. Focusing on keeping your promise will differentiate your organization and create an opportunity for you to ask for more work. Do it consistently.

Of course, customers will make up their own minds about your performance. But, if you and your associates are carrying out your Compelling Focus to consistently deliver your Brand Benefit, you will be far ahead of your competitors. When you tell customers about the good experiences you create for them, you'll get credit. And when you ask for repeat business or referrals at the same time, you will often get them.

Incentives can be useful. Incentives for repeat sales are often discounts. They can also be more creative. Make sure incentives are legal and appropriate for your field. The key isn't the discount or any other incentive; it is demonstrating that you have delivered what you promised.

Incentives for referrals work best when they apply to both the person who makes the referral and the person being referred. A cash reward for customers who make successful referrals and a discount to the persons referred can be effective. By rewarding both the person who makes the referral and the person referred, you create sales and goodwill.

Review the communications and benefits you selected in Step 3 and choose those you can use to tell customers that you are delivering or have delivered a good experience to them. If you don't find any you can use, review the steps in your sales, service, order receipt, and delivery process for opportunities to update customers on delivery, tell them about delivery, or tell them how they can get all the benefits your products and services provide after delivery. Sales and customer service associates often have good ideas about how to do this. Remember, you can tell customers about good experiences using a wide variety of communication techniques, including phone calls, emails, product or service evaluations, and inspections after they take delivery. Check the information they provided on media they like to use in Step 3.

You may find you need to create more good experiences for customers. If so, build them around the fulfillment of your Brand Promise.

Use the Step 9 worksheet in the Worksheets section at the back of this book to write down the good experiences you will communicate, the methods you'll use to communicate them, and any incentives you may offer. Then fill in how you will ask for repeat sales or referrals.

STEP 10

Select the Right Communications

Hundreds of communication techniques exist. Relatively few are right for most organizations. Choosing media and other communication techniques that will be effective with both traditional and new customer types is difficult without selection criteria that help you determine how well each communication method fits into your organization's Process.

In Step 10, you'll make sure media and other communication techniques will help you increase sales and build brand value while avoiding marketing, advertising, and branding pitfalls.

The Step 10 worksheet will help you:

- Evaluate the capabilities of the external and internal media and other communication techniques you are using or could use to deliver your Promise and Proof and to ensure good customer experiences. Then choose the ones that will work together to increase sales and build brand value.

- Determine that your capabilities are ready to handle the responses to your communications methods (i.e. point-of-sale material is on display and includes your Promise and Proof, sales training is completed, and products and services are available).
- Identify and eliminate marketing, advertising, and branding pitfalls before they waste time and money.

Salespeople working with advertising media (i.e. print, outdoor, television, digital, etc.) and other communication techniques (i.e. product videos, sales literature, publicity, etc.) drive a lot of communications and often move it away from what your customers need to know and how they prefer to learn it. Their job is to sell their media or other techniques, not to select and provide the right combination of media and techniques for your organization.

Media salespeople frequently offer "specials" when media isn't selling (for good reasons, such as a time of year). Be careful about specials. Learn *why* the media is on sale.

Some media and communications salespeople can be valuable when they are challenged to provide suggestions on how their products or services can be part of your Process. Take time to meet with those who will listen to you explain your Brand Promise and how you use Brand Proof to make your promise effective with different types of customers. Surprise them by taking them to lunch. You'll quickly learn which ones are listening and are capable of helping you blend increasing sales with building brand value for your organization. You may also learn about trends going on in your field.

Example of a media salesperson's suggestions that fit with the Process

A magazine space salesperson who took the time to understand how Brand Promise and Brand Proof worked for our farm and landscape products client made a suggestion we used effectively for several years. We needed to advertise more frequently but didn't have the budget to buy more advertising, and he suggested we provide products his magazine could use as incentives in their circulation promotions. Our client's Brand Promise and Brand Proof were built into the magazine's circulation promotions and reached thousands of farmers and landscapers. Our expenditure was the wholesale cost of the products they used as prizes in a drawing, a fraction of the cost of the additional advertising we needed.

Some advertising agencies combine different media and communication techniques, looking for crossover between them to increase results (i.e. television and newspaper advertising running at the same time, advertising offering free literature or videos of products in action, advertising linked to an offer on the firm's website, etc.). This can be effective because it increases frequency, audience, and impact. Explore these and other combinations.

Don't be put off when combinations of media and other techniques reach the same customers. The experience of seeing your advertising in several different forms will give your firm credibility as your Brand Promise and Brand Proof are encountered again and again.

Be sure to use publicity opportunities to further build frequency. Employ new product announcements, unusual photographs with captions, awards, new personnel appointments and advancements, by-lined articles, and interviews.

Give special consideration to media and other techniques recommended by associates and customers. This is especially important at the retail level. For example, many farmers are avid readers of local publications that contain listings of used equipment for sale.

Working with firms that provide a range of media and techniques can save your time because you only have to teach your Brand Promise and Brand Proof to one group. However, it is important to remember that these firms are still media and technique driven.

Much of their income comes from producing and buying advertising and producing other communication techniques. Part of their motivation is selling you on what they produce so they can charge for their associates' time, collect commissions from advertising media (usually 15 percent), and mark up the costs of production and other services such as printing (often 15 percent, but could be whatever the market will bear). They may try to offer everything you need in order to capture more of your marketing and advertising dollars. Although convenient, this can have disadvantages. The best people for every assignment aren't always employed by these firms. The best advertising artists, for example, aren't always the best corporate identity artists. The best researchers are not always employed by agencies with a research division.

Sometimes specialty firms or freelancers are more skilled and experienced in completing certain assignments. If you rely on a firm that wants to handle all the different media and communication techniques your firm uses, take the time to make sure they employ people who work in these techniques regularly and successfully. Also make sure that the creative people at the firms who do your work understand and support your Brand Promise and Brand Proof. The key to success, whether working with an agency or outsourcing work yourself, is the same: you must demand your work be done by qualified specialists who understand and work to communicate your Brand Promise and Brand Proof. Doing this is not restricting creativity; it is insisting upon disciplined creativity. Don't let the creativity argument lead you away from the Process's focus on building sales and brand value.

In Step 10, you'll take charge of media and the selection of communication techniques to manage communication rather than allow it to be driven by the people who sell it. This step equips you to evaluate recommendations by media reps, associates, agencies, and others. This evaluation ensures that you utilize the input from your interviews with associates and customers. It helps you select media and communication techniques your customers utilize and encourages you to make sure they work together to communicate your Brand Promise and Brand Proof.

The Capabilities and Readiness Charts

The Capabilities and Readiness Chart – External on the Step 10 worksheet will help you evaluate the capabilities of each external communication technique and medium. It will help you judge them on their ability to:

- Present your Brand Promise
- Communicate your Brand Proof
- Indicate whether this media or technique was recommended by associates
- Deliver examples of good experiences and ask for additional business or referrals
- Connect to your website
- Provide frequency of contact
- Call for action
- Present an offer
- Provide a connection to retail
- Determine cost per traditional customer or new customer reached

Use the Capabilities and Readiness Chart – Internal to evaluate the capabilities of internal media or other internal communication techniques. It will judge them on their ability to:

- Present your Brand Promise
- Communicate your Brand Proof
- Indicate if this media or technique was recommended by associates

- Deliver examples of associates implementing the Compelling Focus
- Provide your website and social media content
- Provide frequency of contact
- Call for action
- Communicate with team members
- Communicate with all associates
- Communicate with distribution
- Recognize associates' contributions.

Invest in media and other communication techniques that score the most check marks (and have an acceptable cost per traditional/new customer reached).

In the evaluation, give special consideration to media and other communication techniques that were recommended by customers. This is especially important at the retail level for lots of small reasons that can pay off. For example, your use of a local media may associate you with its reputation.

Production and media are the biggest expenses in communication. Always keep in mind that media isn't the only way to communicate. The best communication techniques of the past are still the best techniques today:

- Word of mouth
- Good customer experiences combined with requests for additional business or referrals
- Superior service provided by associates and dealer associates
- Performance of products or services and helpful, motivated associates.

You will increase the effectiveness of your communication significantly by delivering good experiences to customers and pointing out these experiences. Advertising or using publicity to communicate good experiences is effective, but don't rely solely on media advertising and publicity to get increased sales and referrals because they don't have the impact of individual messages. Find other ways to communicate directly. Telling customers through direct contact makes them feel special and pays off. If you decide to use customers or associates for advertising and publicity, be sure to get their permission. Check the Step 3 worksheet for what customers and associates said about the ways they prefer to get information.

All communication techniques have their advantages and disadvantages. No matter how exciting a communications technique may be (it may include cute copy, attractive graphics, or be presented by a celebrity), it either communicates your Brand Benefit and Brand Proof or it does not.

As with everything else, there are no silver bullets. Even if a piece of media or a technique generates thousands of inquiries, it can be ineffective unless your sales and distribution organization is ready to turn the interest it generates into sales and then good experiences for customers. Many times, I have seen months-old inquires sitting untouched on dealers' desks. Once, I discovered hundreds of brochures still in their boxes up on a dealer's shelf long after a campaign was concluded. Dealers will use the selling materials you provide more efficiently when they are told the role they play in delivering the Brand Promise and Brand Proof and are aware of how to review them with customers.

Here are some examples of media and communication techniques available today and some of our clients' experiences with them:

Events – Events are about enthusiasm before and during, but usually not afterward. Enthusiasm goes away fast and there is little sponsors can do to prolong it. The buildup and the actual event are what events have to offer. Events salespeople emphasize the value of your organization's association with the event, but it's the audience you must evaluate. Ask about how many traditional customers and how many potential customers will come to the event or will see its promotion or broadcast. The event's potential to communicate your

Brand Benefit and Brand Proof is what you need to understand. Also decide if it represents your Brand Promise.

Events can be effective when your Brand Promise is relevant to the specific audience. A tractor pull with an audience of farmers is a good possibility for a farm equipment manufacturer or dealer.

Another consideration is whether you can tie the event into your sales process. Perhaps your dealers could be involved in promoting it. Look for ways to connect the event to the way you sell and the people who do your selling. Remember, a one-time event can't replace regular, consistent communication, but it could temporarily increase the effectiveness of that communication.

Example of event sponsorships that paid off for sponsors

We helped re-brand the Senior Bowl national football game, secure sponsors and a new television contract, and sell out the stadium in less than six months. We recruited sponsors who covered many of the event's expenses. The sponsors stayed with the game for years because we tied the event into their marketing and sales. Interviews with National Football League coaches and scouts revealed that the game was an important scouting opportunity where they evaluated the best college seniors as they practiced and played against each other. Nationally known NFL coaches and players volunteered to star in the bowl game's advertising and promotions. We reviewed the game's expenses and created sponsorships that covered many of them while providing sponsors with opportunities to combine the game's focus on revealing the best prospects for the NFL draft with their own efforts to serve their customers. Sponsorships were worked out that used the resources and met the needs of the sponsors. A worldwide hotel chain, for example, provided rooms for the players in exchange for exposure in the game's publicity materials and the right to include information about their connection with the bowl game in promotions.

Television Advertising – Television is a visual, intrusive medium. One of its big advantages is motion—movement on the screen attracts and keeps attention.

Today, television audiences are available in huge chunks (the audience of a nationally televised program) or small segments (people who live in rural areas across North America for a local country living show). Television salespeople often tout their wide audiences. They can be impressive, particularly if you offer products or services that meet a wide consumer need and have good distribution. Motion can make television especially effective for many advertisers. If you can use motion to communicate your Brand Promise and Brand Proof (i.e. a homeowner saving time by zipping around her lawn on a zero-turn lawn mower), television can be an excellent choice even for local promotions. However, it is a poor choice if you don't offer an easy way for viewers to respond to your advertising and buy (i.e. distribution, direct response). It is also a poor choice if the audience isn't composed of traditional customers or new customer types. Use your Capabilities and Readiness Chart – External to be sure you are ready to handle responses.

Example of the importance of response mechanisms

A company insisted on doing national television advertising before putting in place a dealer-based program to convert customer interest into sales. Inquiries were strong but sales were few. We helped them get their dealers up to speed. With the products and in-store promotions ready, the same television advertising produced excellent sales results and built the brand's reputation.

Other National Consumer Advertising – National consumer advertising comes in many forms: magazines, national radio shows, and the Internet, to name a few. Some media salespeople present it as the quick solution to everything. Like national television advertising, other national consumer advertising only pays off if your organization is ready to convert the interest it generates into sales. That means you have to have a direct response system or a dealer network or another means of interacting with customers in place, as well as other essentials included in the Capabilities and Readiness Chart – External. National advertising makes sense only when it reaches your customers and potential customers *and* your distribution, sales, and customer service are ready to convert interest to sales.

Example of national consumer advertising media that paid off

National consumer advertising played a big role in expanding the farm and landscaping products brand to consumers in the new country lifestyle market with our client's Zero-Turn Mowers. However, the national consumer advertising we didn't do was as important as that we did. National newspaper advertising was suggested. Customers and potential customers lived in the country and owned large lawns. Dealers were located in rural areas. The newspaper recommended was read mostly by people who lived in cities and suburban settings. We knew the results we would get without even testing—too few real prospects for the cost. That's a major pitfall. By studying all the options, we found television media that reached people who lived in the country and mowed large lawns. Advertising using this medium, coordinated with local promotion by dealers, paid off with increased sales and increased brand value.

Paid-For Editorial – This pitfall often fits into the category of "too good to be true." Although the line between editorial and advertising is blurred (today's talk show hosts and commentators endorse products especially their own), be cautious when contacted about buying editorial that consists of your message delivered so it appears as news rather than as advertising. Readers spot that a mile away.

Example of paid-for editorial that didn't pay off

Contacted by a "television producer" about buying an editorial-style presentation for their business on television monitors located in airports, a client was intrigued by the huge audience claimed and the famous movie and television star billed as the narrator. We recommended against it because the audience included few of this client's customers or new customer types. But the audience numbers promised were too attractive for the firm's management to resist. Lots of up-front money and management time went into reviewing the script, guiding video cameramen about the factory, and finally gathering all the employees together to wave enthusiastically at the camera. The production company went out of business before the video appeared.

"Civic Rent" – Civic rent is the cost of things you are asked to sponsor or advertise in because your organization is run by good citizens. Often, they are sold for the value of their audience. Sometimes the audience can have value. But many times these are mostly donations.

Example of Civic Rent that could have value

Consistent advertising in the local symphony program could pay off for a car dealer with a Brand Promise of superior service and Brand Proof of a service where the dealer picks up customers' cars at their work in the morning, leaves them loaners, services their cars, and returns them before quitting time.

Being in the Movies – The size of the silver screen's audience and the magnificence of the images and surround sound are seductive. But they aren't always effective and don't necessarily help you communicate with potential customers. If you are considering paying for your product to be used in a motion picture, analyze the potential audience carefully to learn how many of these people are your customers or potential customers. Then ask how your Brand Promise and (hopefully) Brand Proof will be presented. A few seconds of your product seen on the silver screen isn't likely to increase sales unless there is a clear connection in the story to your product. Perhaps the most famous example of this was Reese's Pieces in the film *E.T.*-The Extra-Terrestrial. Your product as part of the story could pay off, but this is rare and you will need to find ways to tie your movie appearance into the rest of your communications, such as with dealer promotions.

Publicity – The old adage that it doesn't matter what the media says about you as long as they spell your name right doesn't ring true today. You do care about what they say about you. Publicity that presents your Brand Promise and examples of your Brand Proof is effective. By actually being news (i.e. being mentioned as something new that people need to know about), this kind of publicity (including case histories in business magazines, television interviews, product reviews, by-lined articles) can be effective. An advantage of media publicity over advertising is that there is usually more time and space for Brand Proof in publicity than in advertising. Knowing how your products or services meet current customer needs can help you or your public relations specialist develop news about your products, services, or brand that produces valuable publicity.

Example of the value of Brand Proof in publicity

We used publicity supported by sales literature and a product video to sell out a new farm machine in just a few months. We did no advertising. The product was made newsworthy by identifying the ways it saved energy and moisture as it increased crop yields at a time when world hunger was in the news. A spokesperson (a PhD agronomist trained in the company's Brand Promise and Brand Proof) described in interviews how the product produced higher crop yields and controlled soil erosion. Publicity on television, radio, and in print media in fifteen cities as well as in national publications prompted traditional and new customer types alike to visit dealers who were prepared to sell the new product. One farmer drove over five hundred miles to the factory to make sure he got one. A year's production sold out in a few months.

Build your Brand Promise and Brand Proof into publicity materials. But be careful about it. The media won't run publicity that is just an attempt to get free advertising. Look for opportunities to paraphrase your Brand Promise and present your Brand Proof as useful information for your audience.

Don't worry about using your Brand Promise and Brand Proof over and over again in these materials. Communicating them again and again is what you need. Find creative ways to build them into your publicity techniques. Often the best place is in quotes. Use different media so the information you provide is news to their audiences.

Example of the difference created by Brand Proof in publicity

One of our bank clients hired a new marketing manager. She soon told us she was tired of seeing references to the bank's Brand Promise and Brand Proof built into the news releases we prepared for media in their markets. She didn't realize that building them into the publicity differentiated her organization from other banks. They didn't always survive editing, but many times they did. When we showed her the results—publicity about her bank that included references to its Brand Promise or examples of its Brand Proof, while mentions of other banks included nothing that distinguished them from competitors—she changed her mind. Making the connection requires a little more work, but it is worth it.

World Wide Web – Many websites aren't effective. You can improve your site or launch a new and more effective one by utilizing your Brand Promise and Brand Proof. Lead with your Brand Promise. Remember, it is powerful because it is a promise that appeals to a wide range of customer types. Use Brand Proof that is relevant to different types of customers to prove you deliver on your promise. The combination of your Brand Promise and your Brand Proof creates effective content. Update it frequently.

Good experiences are particularly effective at differentiating your company from your competitors, and are easily presented on a website. We get good results when we highlight these actions on the front pages of websites and provide links that direct visitors to the full reports. Changing this proof frequently keeps the information fresh and gives visitors reasons to come back to your site. Associates' actions that demonstrate them keeping their organization's promise to customers also creates valuable differentiation.

Buying keywords at search engine auctions is an effective way to build your website's audience. Candidates for your keywords (words your customers and potential customers search for) may be chosen from your Brand Promise and Brand Proof.

Optimize your website by building the keywords into your content in ways that make sense to visitors. This sounds easy, but it is specialized work that requires patience and thought. Newswriting and editing experience is helpful. Experience in digital marketing and writing is also important. Hire professionals. Many former journalists work in digital marketing today and are good candidates. Make sure they review your Brand Promise and Brand Proof. Review how they use keywords to optimize your site and make sure it flows.

Another effective way to build your online audience is advertising on social media. Advertisements placed on social media are viewed as users open their accounts. You can choose to buy audiences to market to based on demographics and regions and reach a certain number of viewers over a specific period of time. Results we have experienced with optimization, advertisements, and keywords and phrases are impressive.

Example from a medical practice

We optimized a medical clinic's website and launched advertising and key phrases on their social media accounts. We used their Brand Promise and Brand Proof to develop keywords. Then we worked with a professional group that optimized the website and placed advertising on social media. We selected the firm we worked with because they were digital experts and because they knew the new media and how to write from their journalism experience. Within a month, unique visitors were up 85 percent—the largest gains coming from advertisements and news feed information on their updated social media pages—and click-through rates were as high as 15 percent, with a cost per click of $2.37. We surpassed all our sales goals in the first month and created increased patient volume and brand value month after month and year after year.

Make sure your website is designed for desktops, laptops, notebooks, and cell phones. But demand more than that. Insist that the design and navigation help your visitors relate to your products and services and is graphically attractive and easy to use. The first impression of any website is what it looks like and how easy it is to navigate.

The External Media Analysis and Readiness Chart will help you determine if important tools and other communications criteria can be delivered by external media and the other communication techniques you use now or are considering. Evaluate external media, other communication techniques you are already using, and new possibilities by locating them on the vertical axis (if they aren't listed, add them) of the External Media Analysis and Readiness Chart on the Step 10 worksheet. Then find the capabilities the media/ communication techniques can offer in the horizontal axis at the top of the page. Put a checkmark in the square that aligns the media or communication technique with the capabilities provided by the media or technique.

Some of the capabilities listed in the External Capabilities and Readiness Chart are the same as those listed in the Internal Capabilities and Readiness Chart, although the definitions of these terms vary.

Definitions of the capabilities for the External Chart are listed below:

- **Reaches Traditional Customer Types** describes the circulation or audience of traditional customer types.
- **Reaches New Customer Types** refers to the audience of new customer types.
- **Presents Logo and Brand Promise** is a capability that is required for any media or communications technique you are using/planning to use externally.
- **Presents Brand Proof** is the next most important criteria. Your media/communications techniques should present proof that is relevant to the traditional and new types of customers you are reaching.
- **Presents Good Experiences** means there are space and time to present the experiences of your customers and associates as they follow your Compelling Focus.
- **Connects to Website** means that your audience has quick access to your website. Usually it is best for the link to lead to the webpage describing the subject of your communication.
- **Frequency of Contact** describes how often your traditional customers and new customer types see, read, or hear your communications. Repetition is important in all communications.
- **Call for Action** is a declaration of what the people in your audience should do next. It is often left out. Use it.
- **Presents an Offer** describes content that precipitates actions such as clicking through to your website, visiting a dealer, or contacting your call center.

- **Affordable on Cost/Customer Basis** means determine cost per customer or new customer reached not cost per thousand or another measure of a total audience. Ask how many customers or potential customers the media or communication technique reaches. Then divide that number by the cost of using it. Now make a judgment on how much you are willing to pay to reach this number of customers or potential customers. For example, a new car dealer may decide that everyone who reads the local newspaper over the age of sixteen is a potential car buyer. But are they potential buyers of the type of car the dealer is selling? Are they interested in a new car now? Thinking like this may lead the dealer to a more efficient media or a better deal on media.

- **Connection to Retail** is getting your customer or prospect to a prepared retail contact quickly and easily. It could mean your click-through address in an advertisement takes the interested individual to a page on your website that guides the visitor to their closest dealer, has appealing images of the new product or puts them in touch with a trained individual who can use your Brand Promise and Brand Proof to explain how your product meets their needs.

- **Distribution Ready/Service Ready** means your dealers, phone center, service people, online purchasing systems, warranty registration, etc. are prepared with information about how this product or service meets your customers' needs.

- **Asks for More Business** means that you are ready to inform customers how you are meeting their needs and ask for repeat business as your product or service is used.

- **Asks for Referral** means that you are ready to inform customers how you are meeting their needs and ask for referrals. Always collect email addresses. It is surprising how many companies don't do it.

- **Media Suggested by Customer** refers to media that customers suggested they preferred to receive information through.

The Internal Media Analysis and Readiness Chart will help you determine the capabilities of internal communication techniques and use them. It is set up like the external chart, with the media communication techniques on the horizontal axis and the capabilities on the vertical axis. Some of the capabilities are the same as those on the external chart. Use a checkmark to indicate that a media or communication technique has certain capabilities. For example, do your sales bulletins feature your logo and Brand Promise?

Definitions of the capabilities listed on the internal chart are below:

- **Reaches All Associates** means that all associates are reached by specific techniques.
- **Reaches Distribution** means the material described reaches all your distribution and the right people who work in it.
- **Presents Logo and Brand Promise** is required for any media or communications technique you are using or planning to use internally.
- **Presents Brand Proof** refers to materials and communications methods that present your Brand Proof. All your sales meetings, dealer meetings, sales bulletins, newsletters, events, Agenda and Accomplishment Reports (see the Step 12 worksheets), sales training, videos, and other materials should do this.
- **Presents Good Experiences** refers to the actions your associates take as they follow your Compelling Focus and

take opportunities to attain associate and team recognition (see the Step 12 worksheet).

- **Presents Compelling Focus** means the material described presents examples of associates being guided by your Compelling Focus.
- **Connects to Website** means that the item in question provides information about good experiences by linking to your website.
- **Frequency of Contact** is how often your associates see, read, or hear your communications.
- **Provides Associate Recognition** means the described material communicates associates' actions and attitudes that result in good experiences for customers.
- **Call for Action** is what associates should do next when it is appropriate.
- **Media Suggested by Associates** indicates that associates said they preferred this technique during interviews.

Give some priority to media and communication techniques suggested by associates and customers.

Make sure you choose media that deliver your Brand Promise and Brand Proof to your customers and new customer types over and over again. Repetition is important in all communication.

Pay Attention to Pitfalls Alarms!

Marketing, advertising and branding pitfalls aren't as easy to avoid as you might think. They often come as recommendations from associates and friends. The people who recommend them get excited about what they promise and pass the information along to you without thinking about it very much, perhaps because they saw a competitor doing it and they don't have suitable evaluation criteria. These Pitfall Alarms should help you recognize pitfalls so you can steer away from them. Use the "alarm" indicator below to do a quick check that could save your organization time and money. If an "opportunity" has any of these characteristics, be wary:

- It's free
- They want you to pay in advance
- Easy monthly payments
- Automatic renewal
- They are not a member of a valid professional organization in their field, and no respected organizations or individuals vouch for them
- No financial references or poor reports
- No references you can talk to and verify their credentials and experience
- They use celebrities to market their services
- No specific information on the number of traditional customers and potential customers they can help you reach
- No information about the needs of the customers or demographics they claim to reach
- You wouldn't pay their price if you were paying only for their audience
- It's advertising disguised as editorial
- Sales rep can't explain how their service will increase sales and build brand value
- Sales rep can't show you samples of their work and the results
- They will hire someone to do the work after you sign the contract
- You can't meet and learn the experience of the people who will do the work
- You can't visit their offices and meet their associates
- Individuals who will do the work do not have credentials and experience in the field

- You need to decide today
- They believe branding is accomplished with a logo and artwork.

Once you get used to using the charts regularly, you will know at a glance the media and communication techniques you are using and what they are communicating.

Visit http://www.getrealaboutbranding.com to download sample Media Analysis and Readiness Charts

STEP 11

Set Goals That Motivate Associates

GET REAL goals are for all associates. They keep score of the results of disciplined teamwork. They are simple, obtainable, and clear. They show associates and other stakeholders what can be achieved using the GET REAL Process over a set period of time (usually twelve months).

These goals combine standard business planning factors—opportunities, restraints, the economic environment, financial considerations, status of sales and distribution organizations, production and service capacities, new products and services, new markets—with the new sales and brand-building power of your tools and associates, and are focused on meeting your customers' changing needs.

They guide planning and implementation as they convert your work on the Process into sales and brand value increases. They should reflect the:

- Advantages of everyone in your organization working to make and keep a clear Brand Promise through consistent behavior guided by your Compelling Focus
- Effectiveness of the consistent communication of your Brand Promise and your Brand Proof through the right media and communication techniques and through associate behavior
- Business-building power of communicating good customer experiences to customers and asking for more business or referrals
- Creativity and enthusiasm of associates participating in the development of and progress toward fulfilling Team Objectives (see Step 12) that allow all associates to contribute to accomplishing goals.

These goals are more than just numbers. Like the Brand Benefit and Compelling Focus, they help set the direction of the organization. They also provide guidelines for the allocation of resources and establish measurements of overall accomplishment.

Goals in the Process have a unique format.

Excellence Goals define what your organization will be excellent at communicating (your Brand Benefit, Brand Promise, Brand Proof, and your customers' good experiences).

Review Excellence Goals with both associates and customers. Encourage associates to share them with customers. Let them know these goals take into account input and insights from associates and customers as well as the benefits of the actions and attitudes encouraged by your Compelling Focus. Write these goals in simple language, not "business-speak." Determine how you will measure progress.

Accomplishment Goals measure the elements that drive Excellence Goals. Track progress over twelve month periods. Don't worry about reaching or surpassing them. Start out with modest gains. Increase them as associates learn to work as teams and celebrate progress. You are creating momentum that will last.

Fight the temptation to list too many Accomplishment Goals. Boil them down until you have between four and six short statements that will help you and your associates think, prioritize, and "do." Disciplined thinking (led by an understanding of your customers' current needs) and good prioritizing are vital to choosing Accomplishment Goals as well as for setting Team Objectives with the input of team members (Step 12). "Doing" based on the Compelling Focus will get the sales and brand value results you are seeking.

Many variables are involved in striving to reach goals. Your associates control most of them. Adopt a new way of measuring success. Determine that you will celebrate progress toward your goals rather than the complete attainment of them.

Organizations are composed of people. Customers are people. Human behavior is not 100 percent quantifiable or controllable. Avoid the trap of believing that organizations work like chemical reactions or math formulae; you will not always get the same results. Pursue, measure, and communicate progress toward your Excellence and Accomplishment Goals.

Example of Excellence and Accomplishment Goals for a manufacturer

Excellence Goals

- *Be outstanding at communicating and delivering superior product performance and service.*

Accomplishment Goals

- *Increase market share for core products by 4 percent.*

- *Increase market share for new products by 10 percent.*
- *Maintain current profitability.*
- *Communicate our Brand Promise and Brand Proof in all communications.*

Example of Excellence and Accomplishment Goals for a homebuilder

Excellence Goals

- *Be outstanding at communicating and delivering more square footage and more features for the price as well as a good experience for every customer.*

Accomplishment Goals

- *Close on four hundred houses.*
- *Satisfy all customers at each stage of the building process.*
- *Build all homes within budget.*
- *Deliver good experiences to all customers using checklists.*

Example of Excellence and Accomplishment Goals for a district attorney's office

Excellence Goals

- *Be outstanding at communicating and delivering increased public safety through faster prosecution and crime prevention.*

Accomplishment Goals

- *Speed up justice by reducing the time required to complete cases by 20 percent.*

- *Work with partners to interrupt the processes that lead to criminal behavior—especially among young people—by coordinating help from multiple sources for students suspended from school for exhibiting precursors to violence.*
- *Use technology to improve service, accuracy, efficiency, and to measure improvements.*
- *Share the tools we use against crime with district attorneys across the state and nation.*
- *Communicate progress internally and to the public.*

As you set your goals, keep in mind the new tools you and your associates have to work with as a result of using the Process.

Because of your work in Steps 1 – 10, you are equipped with information and tools you may not have had in the past or, if you did, may not have used to their full potential. The Process has helped you uncover opportunities to reach both traditional and potential customers and to unleash the power of your associates, who are now focused on meeting customers' current needs. In Step 12, you will unlock the full potential of your associates. They are your best communications media. Here's a quick outline of what you and your associates have to work with now:

- One clear definition of your Brand Benefit for all associates and customers, to be used in all communications material
- The power of the ideas, actions, and attitudes produced by associates aiding in the implementation of your Compelling Focus
- The positive effect on customers brought on by keeping your Brand Promise time after time
- Brand Proof that makes your Brand Promise compelling for both traditional and new types of customers
- The increased productivity of all associates due to their application of the Compelling Focus Question when making decisions

- The loyalty and sales results gained by highlighting good experiences to customers as you ask for repeat sales and referrals
- The power of the right combinations of media and other communication techniques selected using the Media Analysis and Readiness Charts
- The money and time savings provided by using the Pitfall Alarms described in Step 10
- The productivity increases that come as associates learn to communicate with each other at team meetings and use your internal communication tools
- Goals that motivate associates
- Good customer experiences to communicate to customers and prospects through your associates, your website, social media, and sales conversations.

Use the Step 11 worksheet in the Worksheets section at the back of this book to set your goals.

STEP 12

Involve All Associates

In this final step, you'll enable and motivate associates to make consistent progress on your organization's goals as they create powerful internal and external communication tools that differentiate your organization, products, and services from competitors. You'll utilize key elements of your Associate Involvement/Communication Plan:

- Excellence Goals
- Accomplishment Goals
- Team Objectives
- Visibility of progress
- Associate communication
- Agenda and Accomplishment Reports
- Group assignments
- Team leaders and team members responsibilities
- Associate and team recognition
- Management support.

A line from Shakespeare's *The Merchant of Venice* has stuck with me over the years because it is so true: "If to do were as easy as to know what were good to do, chapels had been churches and poor men's cottages princes' palaces."

Lack of input into the "to dos", lack of recognition, lack of meaningful measurements and methods of reporting contributions are the reasons many business plans don't get done or only get done with constant prodding. Associates can't contribute to their organization's goals without knowing, participating in, creating, and pursuing the objectives that drive them, seeing the effects of their contributions, learning the desired behavior from peer examples, being recognized for their efforts, and receiving support from management.

In Step 12, you solve this age-old challenge for your organization by creating and maintaining associate involvement through your Associate Involvement/Communications Plan. Using it, you and your associates will be able to identify the "to dos" and make consistent progress toward reaching them as you:

- Determine Team Objectives and make progress on them
- Ask the Compelling Focus Question as you and associates make decisions and interact with each other and customers
- Use the Compelling Focus Question to help select goals, actions, and attitudes that get results by meeting customers' needs
- Document examples of good experiences that have resulted from asking the Compelling Focus Question and share them with team members for review at team meetings
- Recognize associate contributors and cite their contributions
- Communicate to all associates the good associate experiences created by asking the Compelling Focus Question
- Communicate to customers and prospects the good customer experiences produced by asking the Compelling Focus Question

- Use small groups within teams to work on assignments between team meetings and report back (thereby gaining more insight and significantly reducing the time spent in full meetings)
- Provide constant visibility of results on Team Objectives for team members and all associates
- Ask for and receive support from management when needed.

Measurements of progress provide important associate motivation. The **Excellence Goal** of being the best at communicating can be measured by making sure you use media and other communication techniques that deliver your Brand Benefit and Brand Proof to customers and associates as well as meeting other criteria on the Media Analysis and Readiness Charts. One Team Objective could involve using the charts to check every internal and external communication technique you use or are considering using. By doing this, you ensure that media and other communication techniques are effective before you spend money and time on them. Strive for 90 percent of the communication techniques you use to meet at least four criteria. Another objective could be to keep track of the number of times you review the Pitfall Alarms and heed their warnings. Another may be to track the number of times your organization communicates good experiences to customers as you ask for additional orders or referrals. Determine where you are on these measurements and track progress monthly and cumulatively over twelve-month periods.

The Excellence Goal of being the best at delivering your Brand Benefit can be measured by breaking it down into two Accomplishment Goals:

- The delivery of your Brand Promise, with products or services provided on time, complete, in excellent condition, and at the right place (if applicable, make sure it's easy to assemble).

- The delivery of your Brand Benefit through ensuring good customer experiences of your products or services.

Defining and tracking how you reached a high success rate with regards to both these Accomplishment Goals creates data you can use to prove that you consistently keep your Brand Promise. It also produces satisfied customers who will buy again and again as you remind them that you kept your promise.

Accomplishment Goals are measures you may already use. These include sales increases, more business from existing customers, more business from new customers, increased market share, increased productivity, purchasing savings, etc. Break them down into Team Objectives. Consider as a Team Objective consistently paying vendors within ten days of delivery in exchange for them making you a first-served customer (you set the requirements). Years ago, I found an excellent photographer. So good, in fact, that he was always busy. I consistently got to the front of his line by handing him payment at the same moment he handed me the photos.

Team Objectives are measurable actions associates or teams of associates take to contribute to Excellence and Accomplishment Goals. They are determined by team leaders and team members with facilitator and management input. They aren't about everything team members do; rather, they are made up of four to six measurable things associates can do that will drive progress toward the organization's Excellence and Accomplishment Goals. They don't replace what associates already do; they streamline it.

Review the capabilities and communications you selected in the Input Analysis Chart (part of the Step 3 worksheet) and your Excellence and Accomplishment Goals as you work with team leaders and teams to set Team Objectives. Establish twelve-month goals and report monthly and cumulatively.

Use these examples to jump-start your thinking:

Example of Excellence Goals, Accomplishment Goals, and Team Objectives for a homebuilder

Excellence Goals

- Be outstanding at communicating and delivering more square footage and more features for the price, and deliver a good experience for every customer.

Accomplishment Goals

- Close on four hundred houses.
- Satisfy all customers at each stage of the building process.
- Build all homes within budget.

Objectives for Construction Team

- Build four hundred houses.
- Build all houses within budget.
- Ensure 80 percent of customers have good experiences, using checklists to track construction at framing, when homes are completed, and the post-closing period. Ask for referrals at each of these points.

Example of Excellence Goals, Accomplishment Goals, and Team Objectives for a district attorney's office

Excellence Goals

- Be outstanding at communicating and delivering increased public safety through more effective prosecution and crime prevention.

Accomplishment Goals

- *Speed up justice by reducing the time required to complete cases by 20 percent.*
- *Work with partners to interrupt the processes that lead to criminal behavior, especially among young people, by coordinating help for young people suspended from school.*
- *Use technology to improve service, accuracy, and efficiency, and measure improvements.*
- *Share the tools we used against crime with district attorneys across the state and nation.*

Team Objectives for district attorney's juvenile team

- *Intervene with all students suspended from school (and their families) to address discipline problems when violence is indicated.*
- *Identify problems behind bad behaviors and prepare treatment plans that involve the entire family.*
- *Implement and measure the success of the treatment plans through a multi-agency team of social workers, educators, law enforcement professionals, judges, and counselors.*
- *Communicate results to parents, educators, the district attorney, social workers, law enforcement professionals, judges, counselors, and the public through presentations, annual reports, and on-going publicity.*

Visibility of progress toward completing Team Objectives can be created in many ways. Be sure monthly progress is tracked and is readily visible to team members and associates. Visibility can be assured through techniques as simple as posting updates on a wall or as sophisticated as intranet updates. Work with team leaders and members to decide on the visibility methods they will use. If you decide to use an intranet, decide on an internal communication manager who will set it up and keep it up to date.

Examples of visibility of progress toward completing Team Objectives

- *Our point-of-sale printing company client used bulletin boards to provide visibility of progress on objectives and recognition for its manufacturing and sales teams.*
- *The homebuilders' associates also used bulletin boards to track progress on Team Objectives.*
- *A bank client used a monthly newsletter to communicate progress toward objectives and recognize associates' contributions.*
- *The district attorney's office used bulletin boards.*
- *A medical organization used an intranet.*

Communications regarding the progress toward Team Objectives is shared with each associate team and with the leadership team during monthly meetings and through Agenda and Accomplishment Reports (ARs). ARs should contain the accomplishments of the past month and YTD, as well as progress toward objectives. They should also address actions taken by team members and any associates or groups of associates that have been driving objectives using the Compelling Focus Question. Capture and communicate examples of good experiences created. Communication at team meetings is guided by using the ARs as the meeting agenda. Use the AR forms 12E and 12F located in the appendix to take notes during meetings. Align your notes with the agenda subjects so you create your report as the meeting progresses. Review and send the reports to team members and the leadership team and save them for future reference. Used properly, the ARs can literally drive team progress.

(Sample reports and forms are available in the appendix and downloadable at http://www.getrealaboutbranding.com)

Group assignments within teams are important. They make meetings move more quickly and provide time for research, thought, input from non-team members, and preparation of reports for presentation to teams. They are also an opportunity for associates to earn recognition. One person should be chosen to lead each assignment and should choose the team members they want to work with on it.

Example of group assignments

An early group assignment undertaken by the district attorney's Victim Services Team involved capturing the services they provided in a brochure for victims of crime. By putting the services down on paper, a small group of team members defined them and perfected how they were delivered. With input from the entire team, this flyer became the foundation of victim services and successfully communicated an attitude of compassion and reliability, which was then adopted by every associate in the district attorney's office.

Team Leaders' and Members' Responsibilities

The team leaders' and team members' responsibilities should be shared with all associates and available for reference. Being asked to serve on a team is an honor because it says that management has confidence in the associate's experience and ability. Serving on a team brings opportunities as contributions are made and recognition shared.

Examples of team leaders and co-leaders' responsibilities

- *Hold formal meetings at least once a month.*
- *Post the Compelling Focus.*
- *Post Team Objectives and update progress at least monthly.*

- *Review Team Objectives and progress at each meeting.*
- *At meetings, use ARs to set the agenda and take notes.*
- *Following meetings, send completed ARs to team members for input. Then, finalize and send to the leadership team leader for review at the next meeting.*
- *Make group assignments to research, analyze, and make recommendations on specific topics as needed.*
- *Review the results of assignments at team meetings and document in ARs.*
- *Identify and recognize the contributions of individuals and groups of individuals to progress on objectives during team meetings and in ARs.*
- *Ask and answer the Compelling Focus Question in response to any issues that arise and ask members to report how they or other associates used the Compelling Focus Question during the past month to create good experiences for associates or customers. Document in ARs.*
- *Discuss the value of progress on objectives in terms of reaching Accomplishment and Excellence Goals.*
- *Provide all associates with forms that ask the Compelling Focus Question and the results for associates and customers and review returned forms at meetings. Recognize their contributions in internal communications.*

Examples of team members' responsibilities

- *Attend meetings and participate.*
- *Document examples of associates asking the Compelling Focus Question and for any resulting good customer or associate experiences. Bring examples to meetings with names of contributors for recognition.*
- *Accept and participate in assignments and present reports to team.*

- *Review the Team Agenda and Accomplishment Reports circulated following meetings and provide input.*
- *Ask and answer the Compelling Focus Question of yourself and document any good associate or customer experiences that result. Bring to meetings.*

Feedback should be provided by the leadership team to associates regarding progress toward objectives, and leaders should recognize the contributions of high-performing individuals and teams. Recognition should be made clear in ARs and in internal communications.

Recognition can be granted in many different ways. No matter how it is done, it must indicate management's awareness of the team's progress toward objectives, the contributions of the associate or associates involved, and how their actions are consistent with the Compelling Focus and create good experiences for associates and/or customers. Newsletters, an intranet, emails, office visits, and letters sent to associates' homes are all techniques that have been successfully used to provide this feedback. Having team members personally thank associates who contributed is also effective.

The leadership team should select the best examples of associates asking the Compelling Focus Question and record the good experiences the associates in question produced for internal and/or external communications materials.

Examples of associate recognition published by a homebuilding firm for associates and customers

Builder George Wilbur knows his customers become concerned when the weather turns bad. Instead of letting them wonder how it's affecting their building schedule, George calls them in the evenings and updates the schedule. These updates provide customers with good experiences as they are kept informed and their concerns about scheduling delays are addressed before they have to ask.

Builder Robert Smith and Coordinator Julie Ridgeway saved a customer thousands of dollars. While inspecting the customer's lot, Robert noticed that it required a lot of fill. He discussed the problem with the customer and with Julie. Julie helped the customer trade the lot for one that didn't require fill. A potentially bad situation was turned into a good experience for the customer.

"Management support" refers to the support provided by the leadership team and management. It may involve coordination between team leaders, the allocation of assets and resources to help teams make progress on their objectives, and recognition when associates have implemented the Compelling Focus to create good associate and customer experiences. Management support is important for two reasons:

- It provides associate teams with the resources they need to make progress on their Team Objectives.
- It demonstrates that management is behind the Process and supports associate team efforts.

Examples of management support for teams

Support given to the construction team of the homebuilding firm included managers providing information for demonstration checklists, which created good experiences for customers during the building process, and assistance in making sure homes were ready for successful demonstrations. This information, as well as team input, was used in the final checklists.

Support for the teams at the district attorney's office included new operational software and assistance customizing it to fit the teams' processes.

*Support for the sales team of the point-of-sale materials printing company
included improvements in customer information and phone equipment.*

Sequence of the implementation of the Associate Involvement/Communication Plan

Actions in the Associate Involvement/Communication Plan
build upon one another. Use the directions outlined in the Step 12
worksheet to ensure the Process remains consistent. This sequence
produces the best results:

1. Complete your logo and Brand Promise.
2. Complete the worksheets through Step 12.
3. Place your Brand Benefit from Step 4 on the Step 12
    worksheet.
4. Place your Compelling Focus from Step 5 on the Step 12
    worksheet.
5. Place your Brand Promise from Step 6 on the Step 12
    worksheet.
6. Place your Brand Proof from Step 7 on the Step 12 worksheet.
7. Place your Compelling Focus Question from Step 8 on the
    Step 12 worksheet.
8. Place the media and communications techniques you will
    use to communicate good customer experiences, incentives
    you may offer, how you will ask for repeat sales or referrals,
    and good customer experiences you identified in Step 9 on
    the Step 12 worksheet.
9. Place your selected communication techniques from Step 10
    on the Step 12 worksheet.
10. Place your goals from the Step 11 worksheet on the Step 12
    worksheet.
11. Implement your Associate Involvement/Communication
    Plan using the Step 12 worksheets.

All of the above functions can be automated using the GET REAL web-based software available at www.getrealprocess.com.

Your tools and Associate Involvement/Communication Plan are now together in one document. This will help you complete the Step 12 worksheet and implement it while maintaining the connection between what you learned customers need and what you actually do for them and tell them about. I don't know of another process that establishes and maintains this vital connection between knowing what your customers need, fulfilling it, and getting credit for doing it.

General information

The forms in the appendix at the end of this book will help you complete the actions in the Step 12 worksheet:

- Form 12-A will help you modify your existing logo with your Brand Promise or create a new one.
- Form 12-B will document your teams and contact information so it is easy to access and update.
- Form 12-C will help you plan your introductory meeting with associates. It also provides talking points.
- Form 12-D will help you set objectives for the leadership team and associate teams.
- Form 12-E is the Leadership Team Meeting Agenda and Accomplishment Report.
- Form 12-F is the Associate Team Meeting Agenda and Accomplishment Report.
- Form 12-G captures examples of using the Compelling Question and allows you to record the good experiences that result.
- Form 12-H presents the team leaders' responsibilities.

- Form 12-I presents the team members' responsibilities.
- Form 12-J guides planning of the Annual Associate Recognition Event.
- Form 12-K suggests intranet subjects.
- Form 12-L suggests website subjects.

Guidance for facilitators

Facilitator(s) and management should meet initially with all team leaders and co-leaders together. In this meeting, they outline the steps in the Process and the GET REAL tools that have been created. They also review the responsibilities of team leaders and co-leaders; the Agenda and Accomplishment Reports; the organization of the team leader's team and associate teams; the commitment of management to support the process; and the fact that your organization is building a competitive edge by focusing on meeting the current needs of associates, customers, and prospective customers.

Give each team leader and co-leader a copy of the *Get Real About Branding* guide and ask them to read it and write down on the Step 12 worksheet things their team members can do to drive the organization's Accomplishment Goals. Meet with them separately to discuss their suggested Team Objectives.

At the first meeting with each team, ask the team leader to review the suggested Team Objectives and work with team members to help them express their ideas. Capture these in the meeting AR. Meet with the team leaders to finalize Team Objectives and present them at the next meeting.

Service on the teams is voluntary. It provides associates with opportunities to participate in the Process and learn how to use teamwork to meet communication and delivery goals. Future leaders can be identified based partly on their service on teams.

Facilitators attend initial team meetings. Let the team leaders explain the Process and what has been learned and documented using it. Then explain management's commitment to the Process. Work with leaders and members to finalize Team Objectives that will drive Excellence and Accomplishment Goals. Discuss with the team how they will make their progress toward objectives visible.

Associate teams meet monthly to:

- Use the ARs as the meeting agenda (Form 12-E, F) to stay on track with the Process
- Record the Compelling Focus Question and the resulting good experiences for customers (Form 12-G)
- Capture progress on objectives, problems, solutions, and the contributions of teams and individual team members
- Request assistance from management when needed
- Review progress on team assignments, analyze problems, recommend solutions, and hear reports
- Complete Team Agenda and Accomplishments Reports (AR) and send them to team members and team leaders.

The team leader team meets monthly to:

- Select, based on contributions and good customer experiences, associates for recognition. Communicate recognition internally and externally as appropriate.
- Prepare and send recognition to the associate teams
- Determine responses to support requests from associate teams and provide coordination between associate teams
- Publish reports for teams on the progress toward goals and objectives and the contributions of all teams. Provide recognition to all team members.

Facilitator(s) should consistently attend team meetings (you will know which teams need the most attention from the ARs) and should guide all leadership team meetings. Team members learn their responsibilities and the importance of fulfilling them as they witness progress on objectives and see how recognition is determined. They become comfortable thinking alongside their associates and building ideas rather than just pointing out what may be wrong or changing the subject just as a good idea is about to surface. Don't allow one person to dominate. Hear what aggressive people have to say, but don't permit complaints or attacks on others. Everybody is there to identify opportunities and put them to work. Apply the Compelling Focus Question. Team members and all associates will get better and better at helping the organization make and keep its Brand Promise to customers.

If possible, rotate team members every two years. Stagger rotations to keep experienced members on the team.

Associates need to know you are behind them. Don't be surprised if they need to grow into these new responsibilities. Assist team leaders but be sure you are assisting, not dominating.

One of the joys of implementing the Process is witnessing associates who haven't had a chance to contribute in the past experience acceptance and interest when they make suggestions. Some of the best thinking tends to come from associates who previously didn't speak up.

Ask team leaders to always use ARs as meeting agendas and after meetings as reports. Instruct them to take meeting notes on the agenda subjects (taken from ARs), edit them, and circulate them to all team members for their input. Then they should make any necessary updates and send them to the facilitator(s) and the leadership team leader for review at the next meeting. Leaders should strive to make meetings fit into an hour.

Facilitator(s) help team leaders learn to provide recognition and encouragement to members who make contributions. Point out team progress on objectives and explain how it helps drive goals. Recognize teams and associates by citing their contributions toward reaching Team Objectives.

Ask all team members and associates to provide examples of asking the Compelling Focus Question and the good experiences it helped produce. Make sure they identify associates who contributed. Record this information in ARs.

Each year, hold an annual recognition meeting with all team members and associates. One of my clients invited associates who excelled at meeting customer needs to their annual stockholders' meetings and cited the importance of their and every associates' contributions. It had a powerful, positive effect.

Begin updating the Process for the next year by working with team leaders and teams to adjust goals and objectives. Re-interview associates, traditional customers, and new customers and update the worksheets.

Use the Step 12 worksheet in the Worksheets section at the back of this book to implement the GET REAL Process through your Associate Involvement/Communication Plan.

CONCLUSION

Just the Beginning

With the completion of the worksheets, you have created your unique Associate Involvement/Communication Plan. It uses the tools available to build sales and profits simultaneously without you having to spend a fortune on advertising, marketing, or branding. Every step in your plan brings you a step closer to meeting your associates' and customers' current needs as they define them.

Your completed plan (as laid out in the Step 12 worksheet) can be used in many different ways. It can serve as the basis for implementing your business plan; make customer needs and associate motivations part of your strategic plan; deliver effective communication in both traditional and new media; create your own media; utilize the American Business Advantage and use the results to differentiate your organization, products, services, and brand; give you confidence in your communications prior to authorizing the cost; steer you around the many pitfalls of advertising, marketing, and branding; involve every associate in growing your organization's sales and brand; and communicate your effectiveness at understanding and meeting customers' needs to your stakeholders. You now have more to work with than your competitors. You have at your fingertips the knowledge, enthusiasm, and creativity of your associates and customers. Remember, when appealing to Americans, enthusiasm and creativity are especially useful because Americans have a tradition of freedom that pays off for individuals as well as society. You, your associates, and your customers are ready to benefit from that tradition.

It is important to consistently implement the Process. Be consistent but also flexible. Use your new tools to build your sales and brand value simultaneously. I want you to succeed. If you decide you want assistance, email me and describe your situation using the contact page at the GET REAL Process website (www.getrealprocess.com) and we will explore how I may be able to assist you.

My hope is that the Process will help you and your organization succeed in today's environment and help America maintain its freedom-based position as the leader in the world economy. I'd be grateful to hear how the Process has worked for you and about any lessons you learned. I may even use them to update the Process.

Art Forward

P. S. I hope you will consider saving your time and getting results faster by scheduling a GET REAL Kick-Start Seminar. You'll be an expert at using the Process and the software in one very interesting day.

GLOSSARY OF PROCESS TERMS

GET REAL means make the perspective and thinking of your associates and customers play a key role in your marketing, advertising and branding.

12 Steps are the twelve connected steps that guide disciplined creative thinking in the GET REAL Process.

12 Worksheets are the worksheets at the end of each step that produce your custom marketing tools that help you and your associates make decisions that build sales and brand value now and for years to come.

Accomplishment Goals measure progress on the items that drive your Excellence Goal.

The **Associate Involvement/Communication Plan** makes you and your associates partners in implementing the Process by involving associates in research, goals, and team efforts so as to make continuous progress on Accomplishment and Excellence Goals.

Agenda and Accomplishment Reports provide the format and subjects of team meetings and, when used to take notes at team meetings, are a convenient and effective way to communicate with team members and other teams. They are at the heart of the Associate Involvement/Communication Plan and keep it moving and on track.

The **American Business Advantage** is the motivation of self-interest that is part of American life. It is harnessed by the Process to motivate associates to deliver the attitude, actions, products, and services that meet customer needs.

Associate and Customer Selection Criteria tells you how to determine which associates and customers can provide input and insights into their current needs and how your organization can meet them.

Associate and Customer Information Selection Criteria tell you how to determine valuable input and insights from associates and customers.

Associate/Customer Interview Questions are questions for associates and customers that elicit thoughtful answers by stimulating their thinking.

Benefits are the immediate and long-term improvements customers and potential customers will receive through your products, services, and follow-up communications.

The **Brand Benefit** is the overarching benefit your products, services and associates deliver to customers.

The **Brand Promise** is your promise that your products, services, associates, and brand deliver your Brand Benefit to customers.

The **Brand Proof** refers to facts that demonstrate how your products, services, associates, and brand keep your Brand Promise for traditional and new types of customers.

Capabilities are the resources (people and things) you have at your disposal now or could have in the future to meet customers' and potential customers' needs.

The **Capability and Readiness Chart** helps you determine which media and other communication techniques have the capabilities to pay off for your organization and are ready to use. Use it to evaluate media and communication techniques you are using or considering using.

Communication – Information is information customers need to make the decision to buy from you, continue to buy from you, or buy more from you.

Communication – Media are the media through which customers and new customers prefer to receive information about your company, products, and services.

The **Compelling Focus** is your firm's definition of how you and your associates behave so as to consistently deliver your Brand Benefit to customers.

The **Compelling Focus Question** is the question you and your associates ask yourselves and each other to make sure all decisions help implement your Compelling Focus. Examples of associates asking the question and the consequent results should be shared regularly with associates.

Connection to Customer Needs refers to the application of information gained from associates and customers through the Process and through your GET REAL tools.

Customers are people and business entities you or your associates can create benefits for, including traditional customers, new types of customers, and people who influence customers.

Disciplined Creativity is creativity focused on communicating and delivering your Brand Benefit through marketing, advertising, branding, research, development, sales, service, engineering, distribution, and other disciplines.

Examples are the author's first-hand experiences of using the principles of the Process over thirty-plus years to simultaneously build sales and brand value. They are indicated by italics.

Your **Excellence Goal** is what your organization aims to be excellent at communicating and delivering.

The **External Media Analysis and Readiness Chart** guides you in choosing effective exterior media and communication techniques and making sure they are in place before launching programs.

The **Internal Media Analysis and Readiness Chart** guides you in choosing internal media and other communications techniques and using them to support programs.

Facilitator(s) are people who, after reading *GET REAL About Branding* and completing the *GET REAL Kick Start Training,* help determine which associates, customers, and new customers to interview; use selected interview questions to gather input; apply the analysis tools and worksheets to create the GET REAL tools; and use the Associate Involvement/Communication Plan to implement the Process.

The **GET REAL Process** is the copyrighted process of gathering and using information from associates and customers to consistently increase sales and brand value by meeting the needs of current and new customers without wasting money on marketing, advertising, and branding pitfalls.

The **Input and Insight Analysis Chart** helps you identify useful information during interviews, select the most important insights, and understand the relationships between individual pieces of information. It prepares you to write your unique Brand Benefit based on meeting the changing needs of customers.

Insights are new perspectives, new customer/associate motivations, new opportunities, and useful pieces of information you either didn't previously know about or knew about but weren't using.

Interviewee Characteristics are the characteristics of associates and customers that make them good candidates for interviews.

Interview Techniques include your demeanor, the clothing you wear, your pledge to do no harm, and the confidentiality you promise to interviewees when conducting interviews.

Needs are what associates and customers report they need today in their work and personal lives. Pay close attention to how they may be different from past needs.

The **Now Period** is the period of time in which specific needs are held by customers and prospects.

Pitfall Alarms help you identify marketing, advertising, and branding pitfalls before they cost money and waste time.

Standard Research Information refers to widely used research questions designed to provide binary answers that often miss valuable customer and associate input and insights.

Team Objectives break down Accomplishment Goals into measurable actions that individuals and groups can make to contribute to reaching the goals. They produce the results.

GET REAL Tools are the valuable marketing tools you develop and use as you complete the twelve worksheets and apply them to building sales and brand value.

Undisciplined Creativity is the practice of relying on short-term slogans; themes; taglines; colorful graphics; and other marketing, advertising, and branding techniques alone to build sales and brand value.

Your Input is capturing your experience and thinking as you work through the Process.

WORKSHEETS

The following worksheets will guide you through the GET REAL Process. In most cases, the versions printed in this book are suitable only for samples; they are probably not adequate to contain all the information you will want to collect. You can find downloadable versions of these worksheets at http://online.getrealprocess.com. Completing the worksheets will build the core of your Associate Involvement/Communication Plan.

As well as digital versions of these worksheets, other useful tools can be accessed by subscribing at the GET REAL About Branding® website-based software (www.getrealprocess.com). The digital software saves a tremendous amount of time and facilitates your thinking, planning, and actions. It moves the information you complete from worksheet to worksheet and updates automatically as you make changes. I worked for years without the digital program. It cuts the time it takes me to work through the Process by 50 percent or more. They can do the same for you. If you choose to request guidance, you can authorize me to look at your worksheets and make suggestions. Visit http://www.getrealprocess.com to learn more about assistance options.

Step 1 Worksheet – Identify Interview Sources

Associates and Others for Interview			
Name/Position	Contact	Phone	Email
Customers for Interview			
Name/Position/Company	Contact	Phone	Email

Step 2 Worksheet – Interview Associates and Customers

Interviewee Information

Name: _____ Associate/Customer

Company: _____

Position: _____

Address: _____

Phone: _____

Email: _____

Interview Date: _____

Interview Location: _____

Tag your interview notes using the following designators during or immediately after the interview:

CUST (Customer), NEED (Need), CAPS (Capabilities), COMS-1 (Media or Communication Technique) or COMS-2 (Information), BENS (Benefits), YOUR (Your Input)

Notes:

Step 3 Worksheet – Analyze Interviews

Part 1 – Refine Data

In the following grids, list all of the information you tagged in your Step 2 interview notes. Put a checkmark in the opportunity column for the items you will use.

CUST (Customers)

Opportunity	Tagged Data	Customer Type	Source
		Existing/New Type	
		Existing/New Type	
		Existing/New Type	
		Existing/New Type	
		Existing/New Type	
		Existing/New Type	
		Existing/New Type	

NEED (Needs)

Opportunity	Tagged Data	Source

CAPS (Capabilities)

Opportunity	Tagged Data	Source

COMS (Communications)

Opportunity	Tagged Data	Communications Type	Source
		Information/Media	
		Information/Media	
		Information/Media	
		Information/Media	
		Information/Media	
		Information/Media	
		Information/Media	
		Information/Media	
		Information/Media	

BENS (Benefits)

Opportunity	Tagged Data	Source

YOUR (Your Input)

Opportunity	Tagged Data	Source

Part 2 – Organize Data

Using the following grids, list your existing and potential customers and, using the tagged opportunities from Part 1, list the NEEDS, CAPS, COMS, BENS, and YOUR categories that apply to each.

Existing Customers

Customer Name	NEEDS	CAPS	COMS-Information	COMS-Media	BENS	YOUR

Potential Customers

Customer Name	NEEDS	CAPS	COMS-Information	COMS-Media	BENS	YOUR

Step 4 Worksheet – Identify Your Brand Benefit

Your Brand Benefit is the benefit your products, services, associates, and brand deliver to customers.

List the Benefit (BENS) opportunities you selected in Step 3 here:

Referring to your benefits information (BENS), write drafts of your Brand Benefit here:

Write your Brand Benefit here:

Step 5 Worksheet – Define Your Compelling Focus

Your Compelling Focus is the definition of how you and your associates behave to consistently deliver your Brand Benefit to customers. Using the Brand Benefit determined in the Step 4 worksheet, write drafts of how the people of your organization will behave to deliver your Brand Benefit below. Begin your statement with the words: "The people of [your organization]…"

Write your Brand Benefit here:

Write drafts of your Compelling Focus here:

The people of _____

Write your edited Compelling Focus here:

The people of _____

Step 6 Worksheet – Create Your Brand Promise

Your Brand Promise is your promise that your products, services, or brand will deliver your Brand Benefit to customers. Study your Brand Benefit and your Compelling Focus as you write drafts of your Brand Promise below.

Write you Brand Benefit here:

Write your Compelling Focus here:

Write drafts of your Brand Promise here:

Write your edited Brand Promise here:

Place your logo and Promise artwork here (see Form 12-A):

Step 7 Worksheet – Define Your Brand Proof

Your Brand Proof is a collection of facts that make your Brand Promise relevant to different kinds of customers. Using the Brand Promise determined in the Step 6 worksheet and the selected "Communication – Information" opportunities from the Step 3 worksheet, write drafts of facts that demonstrate how your promise is relevant to meeting the current needs of customers and prospective customers. You will use this information to define your Brand Proof. You will collect even more Brand Proof in Step 8 that you may append to this document at a later time.

Write your Brand Promise here:

List the Communication – Information opportunities you selected in Step 3 here:

Write examples of your Brand Proof from "Communication – Information" here:

Write your edited Brand Proof here:

Step 8 Worksheet – Ask the Compelling Focus Question

The Compelling Focus Question is the question you and your associates ask and answer to make sure all decisions support the promise and delivery of your Brand Benefit. Ask the Compelling Focus Question and encourage associates to ask it and tell you about the results.

Write your Compelling Focus here:

Write your Compelling Focus Question here:

How does this decision/action/attitude implement our Compelling Focus?

List situations or decisions below and explain how you could apply your Compelling Focus:

Situation #1 _____

Answer: _____

_____

_____

Good experiences resulting for associate(s):

_____

_____

Good experiences resulting for customer(s):

_____

_____

Situation #2 _____

Answer: _____

_____

_____

Good experiences resulting for associate(s):

_____

_____

Good experiences resulting for customer(s):

_____

_____

Situation #3 _____

Answer: _____

_____

_____

Good experiences resulting for associate(s):

_____

_____

Good experiences resulting for customer(s):

_____

_____

Situation #4 _____

Answer: _____

_____

_____

_____

Good experiences resulting for associate(s):

_____

_____

Good experiences resulting for customer(s):

_____

_____

Situation #5 _____

Answer: _____

_____

_____

Good experiences resulting for associate(s):

_____

_____

Good experiences resulting for customer(s):

_____

_____

In Step 12 you will learn the effective ways to motivate all associates by recognizing those who use the Compelling Focus to create good experiences for other associates and customers.

Step 9 Worksheet – Build Repeat Sales and Referrals

Using the tagged "Communication – Media" opportunities from the Step 3 worksheet to stimulate your thinking, write the media and communication techniques you will use to tell your customers about benefits your products and services are providing to them.

List the Communication – (COMS) Media opportunities you selected in Step 3 worksheet here:

| |
| |
| |
| |
| |
| |
| |
| |
| |
| |
| |
| |
| |

List good customer experiences collected using the Step 8 worksheet to communicate:

| |
| |
| |
| |
| |
| |
| |
| |

Choose the media or other communication technique you will use to communicate good experiences to customers.

List incentives you may offer (make sure they are legal and acceptable in your industry):

List how you will ask for repeat sales or referrals:

List how you will follow up:

Step 10 Worksheet – Select the Right Communications

Avoid costly marketing, advertising, and branding pitfalls by utilizing the Capabilities and Readiness Charts and the list of Pitfall Alarms.

External Analysis and Readiness Chart

(Chart is available for download at http://online.getrealprocess.com)

Internal Analysis and Readiness Chart

(Chart is available for download at http://online.getrealprocess.com)

Place the media you selected using the External Analysis and Readiness Chart here:

Place the media you selected using the Internal Analysis and Readiness Chart here (review of Pitfall Alarms):

Step 11 Worksheet – Set Goals That Motivate Associates

The Excellence Goals define what your organization will be excellent at communicating (your Brand Promise and Brand Proof, including your customers' good experiences) and delivering (your Brand Benefit). The Accomplishment Goals measure your organization's progress toward reaching communication and delivery objectives over a twelve-month period.

Write your Brand Benefit here:

Keeping your Brand Benefit in mind, list your ideas for Excellence Goals here:

Goal	Goal Date	Progress

Keeping your Excellence Goals in mind list your Accomplishment Goals here:

Goal	Goal Date	Progress

Finalize your Excellence Goals here by completing this statement:

The people of _____ will be excellent at communicating _____ and delivering _____.

Finalize your Accomplishment Goals that will drive your Excellence Goals here in bullet format:

- _____
- _____
- _____
- _____
- _____
- _____

Step 12 Worksheet – Involve All Associates

Now make the GET REAL Process pay off. Involve all associates in meeting your customers' needs better than your competition and communicate your successes to your associates and customers.

Place your Brand Benefit from Step 4 here:

Place your Compelling Focus from Step 5 here:

Place your Brand Promise from Step 6 here:

Place your Brand Proof from Step 7 here:

Place your Compelling Focus Question from Step 8 here:

Place the good customer experiences you will communicate to customers from Step 9 here:

Place the media you selected to communicate to customers using your External and Internal Media Analysis and Readiness Charts in Step 10 here:

External:

Internal:

Place your GET REAL goals from Step 11 here:

(see Form 12-A):

Determine your teams and team leaders and place them here or use Form 12-B:

Meet with all associates to review the Process, team concept, teams, team leaders' responsibilities, team members' responsibilities, Excellence Goals, Accomplishment Goals, and Team Objectives (see Form 12-C with presentation talking points).

Meet individually with team leaders to discuss Excellence and Accomplishment Goals, set initial Team Objectives, and review how to use Team Agenda and Accomplishment Reports (see Forms 12-D).

Assist individual associate teams as they meet to review initial Team Objectives and provide input on progress. From there, select visibility techniques and record them in Agenda and Accomplishments Reports (Forms 12-D , E, and F).

Associate teams meet at least monthly and use Team Agenda and Accomplishment Reports as meeting agendas. Review objectives, progress, problems, solutions, the contributions of teams and team members, and the assistance needed from management and other teams. Allocate assignments to team members, analyze problems and recommend solutions, hear reports of group members, complete Agenda and Accomplishments Reports, review with associates, and send information to the leadership team (see Forms 12-E and F).

The team leaders should meet at least monthly to select contributions and good customer experiences for recognition; prepare and send recognition to teams and individuals; determine support for teams and provide coordination between teams; publish reports for teams on progress toward goals and objectives, contributions by teams, and team member recognition; and select information on contributions by team members and good experiences they created that should be communicated to associates and customers through e-mails, your website, social media, or other communication techniques. (see Form 12-E and F)

Ask for examples of the Compelling Focus Question being used and for examples that resulted in good experiences for associates and/or customers. Provide the Compelling Focus Question/ good experience forms to all members (Form 12-G) and all associates and ask for feedback at all meetings. Record positive results of asking the Compelling Focus Question on ARs and include recognition from team leadership (to be sent to associate teams and the internal communications manager/webmaster) (Forms 12-E and F).

The leadership team should post and follow team leaders' responsibilities (Form 12-H).

Associate teams post and follow team members' responsibilities (Form 12-I).

The leadership team uses Form 12–J to organize the Associate Accomplishments Annual Recognition Meeting. The internal communications manager provides a summary of contributions and their effects on Accomplishment Goals and Excellence Goals to all associates through an intranet (Form 12-K).

The webmaster hosts selected examples of good customer experiences on your company website (Form 12-L).

APPENDIX

Form 12-A

Logo and Brand Promise Artwork

Criteria: a symbol that represents the Brand Benefit and that applies to all products and services offered. Alternatively, an artwork of letters with type style that matches customers' needs, the industry, and the current Now Period. Size should be effective in both small and large formats. Consider the suggestion of movement. Design with and without prominent Brand Promise.

Modify existing logo:

Create new logo:

Logo as JPEG:

Logo with Brand Promise as JPEG:

Form 12-B

Team Leaders, Members, and Meeting Schedules

Facilitator(s) work with management and human resources to select a leadership team, associate team leaders, and co-leaders (associate team leaders become members of the leadership team and work alongside other individuals who can assist associate teams). Select an internal communication coordinator and webmaster to serve on the leadership team if you don't already have these positions filled.

Facilitator(s) work with team leaders individually to select team members based on their abilities to contribute to the Process. They also develop tentative Team Objectives and ensure team visibility techniques are in operation. Schedule a recognition event twelve months after launch.

Determine Facilitator(s); Leadership Team, Associate Team Leaders, Co-Leaders, and Members.
Facilitator(s):

| |
| |
| |
| |

Teams

Team #1 name: _____
Leader (contact info): _____
Co-leader (contact info): _____

Members	Contact Info

Team #2 name: _____

Leader (contact info): _____

Co-leader (contact info): _____

Members	Contact Info

Team #3 name: _____

Leader (contact info): _____

Co-leader (contact info): _____

Members	Contact Info

Team #4 name: _____

Leader (contact info): _____

Co-leader (contact info): _____

Members	Contact Info

Team #5 name: _____

Leader (contact info): _____

Co-leader (contact info): _____

Members	Contact Info

Internal communication manager (leadership team):

_____

Webmaster (leadership team): _____

Initial meeting date (as an organization or separately as individual teams): _____

Meeting dates, times, and places:

Team	Meeting Date	Meeting Time	Meeting Place

Associate and leadership team meeting schedules

Name	Meeting Date	Meeting Time	Meeting Place

Recognition event schedule

Form 12-C

Meeting to Introduce the Process to Associates

All associates meet with facilitator(s) and team leaders to review the Process. They will learn how the teams and other associates will use the Compelling Focus Question to create good experiences for customers and associates, as well as how these good experiences can be communicated internally and externally. Other topics covered include leaders' responsibilities and initial team meeting dates.

Point Outline for Introductory Meeting with All Associates

- People are our greatest assets.
- These people are you and our customers.
- Meeting associate and customer needs is the reason for the organization.
- Associate and customer needs change as the environment they live and work in changes.
- Nobody knows associates and customers' current needs better than you and our customers.
- We have embarked on a process to make sure we always understand our associates and customers' needs. We need them to know that we are excellent at delivering the benefits of our products and services. We must show our associates and customers that we perform better than our competitors.
- We are doing this through the Process outlined in the book *GET REAL About Branding*.
- The Process was developed by a consulting firm that has helped many clients build their sales and brand value simultaneously by encouraging them to understand their customers and prospective customers' current needs. These client companies then promise customers they will meet

these needs, prove they can meet them, deliver on their promises, and ask for more business and referrals.

- It uses the best communication media in the world—you, your attitudes, and your actions.
- We have asked associates and customers about their needs; lined up our capabilities to meet them; and documented our Brand Benefit, Compelling Focus, Brand Promise, and Brand Proof.
- Your needs that help us build sales and brand value:
- Our customers' needs that can be met by our products, services, brands:
- Our Brand Benefit:
- Our Compelling Focus:
- Our Brand Promise:
- Our Brand Proof (how we keep or will keep our promise and how it is relevant to the current needs of traditional customers and new types of customers alike):
- Our goals, which represent what we can do when everyone focuses on meeting our customers and new customers' needs.

  o Excellence Goals
  o Accomplishment Goals
  o Team Objectives

- We have formed teams in key areas of the organization to develop and implement Team Objectives
- These include the leadership team, which is composed of the leaders of the associate teams and key people from management who can help support them. They are:
- We are choosing associates to serve in associate teams for the first year. You can apply for positions on the teams.
- Associate teams will work with our facilitator(s) and managers to create Team Objectives that will drive our goals.

- The Process is our opportunity to build our sales, our brand(s), our organization's future, and our individual futures by unleashing your training, talents, and determination as we use your ideas and the ideas of our customers to outpace our competitors.

Form 12-D

Work with Team Leaders to Review Excellence and Accomplishment Goals and Set Tentative Team Objectives:

- Review Excellence Goals.
- Review Accomplishment Goals.
- Select objectives for the leadership team that will support associate teams and drive Excellence Goals and Accomplishment Goals.
- Choose four to six Team Objectives that will drive Excellence Goals and Accomplishment Goals.
- Review Accomplishment Agenda and Reports and set up internal and external communications to provide recognition to contributors and show progress on Team Objectives.

_____Team
Objectives and their measurements

_____Team
Objectives and their measurements

_____Team

Objectives and their measurements

_____Team

Objectives and their measurements

_____Team

Objectives and their measurements

_____Team

Objectives and their measurements

Form 12-E

Leadership Team Agenda and Accomplishment Report (AR)

Date of meeting: _____

The team leader reviews the leadership team's objectives and the progress toward reaching them for the past month and cumulatively (record here prior to meeting):

Each associate team leader reviews their team's progress toward their Team Objectives and communicates the best three examples of associates asking the Compelling Focus Question and producing good experiences for associates and customers. Team members determine which reports (including those of individuals who contributed) will be sent for publication on the intranet and which will be sent for publication on the website (record here during meeting):

Each associate team leader whose team has been provided with assistance from the leadership team reports on how this assistance was put to use and the results (record here during meeting):

Non-associate team leaders serving on the leadership team report how they and their associates asked the Compelling Focus Question and discuss any good experiences that resulted (record here during meeting):

The leadership team sends recognition to those who've applied the Compelling Focus Question and to those whose contributions will be published in internal or external communications (following meeting):

The leadership team reviews requests for assistance, decides on what can be provided, and delivers it through the associate team leaders:

Group assignment reports:

New group assignments:

Date of next meeting:

Date AR sent to associate team leaders

Form 12-F

Associate Teams Agenda and Accomplishment Report Form (AR)

_____ Team Agenda and Accomplishment Report

Date of meeting: _____

The team leader reviews Team Objectives and progress on them for the past month and cumulatively (record here prior to meeting):

Each associate team member reports examples of their team members and other associates using the Compelling Focus Question and discusses the resultant good experiences for associates and customers (record here during meeting):

Team members report the contributions of their team and other associates (record here during meeting):

Team members select the three best examples of associates using the Compelling Focus Question (and the resultant good experiences) to be communicated to the leadership team on the Agenda and Accomplishments Report (AR):

Group assignment coordinators report progress on assignments (record here during meeting):

New assignments are made and new group coordinators named (record here during meting):

Team leader reviews assistance provided by leadership team since last meeting (record prior to meeting):

Date of next meeting: _____

Date AR sent to team members and leadership team:

_____

Form 12-G

Compelling Focus Question/Good Experience Form

Compelling Focus Question: how can I (we) make my (our) decision/ action an example of the delivery of our Compelling Focus?

My (our) answer:

Actions taken:

Good experience(s) that resulted for:

    Associate(s) involved:

    Customer(s) involved:

Contributors:

    Names:

    How they contributed:

Form 12-H

Team Leaders' Responsibilities

1. Hold formal meetings at least once a month.
2. Post the Compelling Focus.
3. Post Team Objectives and update with progress at least monthly.
4. Review Team Objectives and progress at each meeting.
5. Use Agenda and Accomplishment Reports to set team meeting agenda, take notes, and create the next AR.
6. Following meetings, send Agenda and Accomplishment Reports to team members for input. Finalize ARs and send them to the leadership team leader for review prior to and at the next meeting.
7. Make group assignments to research, analyze, and make recommendations on specific topics at the next meeting.
8. With the team, select the best three examples of asking the Compelling Focus Question and the resultant good experiences for each associate team. Certify all qualified examples for intranet or website publication and provide direct recognition for individuals who contributed to these examples.
9. Ask the Compelling Focus Question about issues and ask members to report how they and other associates used the Compelling Focus Question during the past month and comment on the good experiences that resulted.
10. Recognize contributors by contacting them directly via e-mail and "in the hall" or office visits.
11. Provide all associates with forms asking about the Compelling Focus Question and review returned forms prior to meetings.

Form 12-I

Team Members' Responsibilities

1. Attend meetings and participate.
2. Talk to associates and ask for examples of them or others asking the Compelling Focus Question. Communicate the resultant good experiences to associates and customers.
3. Bring examples to meetings with the names of contributors and the details of how they contributed. Grant recognition and review them.
4. Participate in group assignments.
5. Ask the Compelling Focus Question and record how it helps produce good experiences.
6. Provide all associates with forms asking about the Compelling Focus Question and review returned forms prior to meetings and at meetings.

Form 12-J

Associate Accomplishments Annual Recognition Meeting

Report on:

- The organization's progress on Excellence and Accomplishment Goals
- The effects on the organization of associates asking the Compelling Focus Question and the resultant good experiences.

Make sure:

- Associate team leaders introduce their members and review their progress on Team Objectives
- Associate team leaders cite their team's best examples of associates asking the Compelling Focus Question and the resulting good experiences
- Leadership team leaders introduce their members and review their progress on Team Objectives. Ensure they cite their best examples of associates asking the Compelling Focus Question and the resulting good experiences
- Management presents awards to associates who created the three best examples of asking the Compelling Focus Question and producing good experiences over the past twelve months
- Management reads the names of everyone who submitted a Compelling Focus Question and good experience and was selected for internal and/or external communication
- To announce Excellence Goals and Accomplishment Goals for the next twelve months.
- To ask teams to review their Team Objectives and revise as necessary.

Form 12-K

Intranet Subjects

1. Logo and Promise.

2. Name of Intranet – "Meeting Our Associates and Customers' Needs."

3. Progress on Excellence Goals.
   a. List progress on Accomplishment Goals.

4. Message from CEO, general manager, or another top leader.
   a. "You're Making It Work."
   b. Summary of contributions, good customer and associate experiences, and progress toward Accomplishment and Excellence Goals.

5. Message from your facilitator.
   a. How associates are learning the Process and making it pay off for the organization. Detail the recognition they are receiving.

6. Team Progress
   a. Monthly reports on each team's progress on their objectives.

7. Each team produce a paragraph-sized report of the three best examples of associates asking the Compelling Focus Question and the resultant good customer and associate experiences.

8. All the qualified examples for the month for each team.

Form 12–L

Website Subjects

1. Special section that serves as an intranet.

2. Front page link – "Learn How We Keep Our Promise."

3. Link content – "Keeping Our Promise."

   a. List examples of good customer experiences created by our associates.